W9-AHC-246

DATE DUE		
MAY 1 4 1996		
MAY 1 6 1996		

CHILD LABOR

LAURA OFFENHARTZ GREENE

CHILD LABOR: THEN AND NOW

An Impact Book
Franklin Watts
New York ◆ Chicago ◆ London ◆ Toronto ◆ Sydney

for M. M. and M. Berger,
the newest members of my family

Photographs copyright ©: AP/Wide World Photos: pp. 8 top, 92; UPI/Bettmann
Newsphotos: pp. 8 bottom, 118 top; The Bettmann Archive: pp. 12, 16 top, 22,
28; North Wind Picture Archive, Alfred, ME: pp. 16 bottom, 26, 30; New York
Public Library, Rare Print Collection: pp. 33, 39, 40, 44, 50 top,
51, 53, 54, 56, 57, 59, 60; International Museum of Photography at George
Eastman House: p. 48; Milwaukee Art Museum, Gift of Robert Mann: pp. 50
bottom, 61; Impact Visuals: pp. 79 (Cara Metz), 81 (D. Steele), 88, 90 top
(both Lonny Shavelson), 90 bottom (Philip Decker); UNICEF: pp. 114 (Dennis
Budd Gray), 118 bottom (Sean Sprague), 121 top (Francene Keery), 121 bottom
(Yann Gamblin); Monkmeyer Press Photo: p. 83 (Mimi Forsyth).

Library of Congress Cataloging-in-Publication Data

Greene, Laura Offenhartz.
Child labor : then and now / Laura Offenhartz Greene.
    p.   cm. — (An Impact book)
Includes bibliograhical references and index.
Summary: Surveys the history of child labor and its abuses and
examines what has been done to eliminate the exploitation of
children at work.
    ISBN 0-531-13008-8
    1. Children—Employment—United States—History—Juvenile
literature. 2. Children—Employment—Government policy—United
States—History—Juvenile literature. 3. Children—Employment-
-Juvenile literature. [1. Children—Employment—History.]
I. Title.
HD6231.G74   1992
331.3′1′0973—dc20   92-17721 CIP AC

CONTENTS

O N E

THE
PROBLEM
AND
ITS HISTORY

How long, O cruel nation, will you stand, to move the world, on a child's heart.
—Elizabeth Browning, "The Cry of the Children," 1843

One evening at dusk, Mary Poppins, the Banks children, Bert the chimney sweep, and his fellow workers joyfully danced and sang across the rooftops of London. This musical, acrobatic scene in the 1964 motion picture *Mary Poppins* glorified the life of a chimney sweep. In typical Hollywood fashion the movie depicted the charms and brotherhood of the vocation. The description is attractive, one we want to believe and wish were true.

The real life of an English chimney sweep was much different. It was extremely arduous and filled with terror. A sweep could fall off a roof, get burned, or become sick from years of inhaling smoke and soot. Most sweeps were actually children. Their adult employers forced them to

Left: *A scene from* Mary Poppins, *a movie that glamorized the life of a chimney sweep*

Below: *A modern-day chimney sweep working in the Boston area*

work until their hearts and young bodies cried out in pain. Jonas Hanway's letter to a London clergyman in 1785 gives a hint of their true working environment. "It is beyond dispute," he wrote, "that no employment [as a sweep] in civil life, exercised by persons of so tender an age is learned with so much pain and difficulty...."[1]

Three years later James Dunn, master chimney sweep at Knightsbridge, more fully described the lives of these "climbing boys," as the sweeps were sometimes called. An entry in the minutes of the British House of Commons recorded his concerns: "That great Inhumanity is practiced by Masters on their Apprentices—That he himself had been very ill-treated by his Master, having been bound Apprentice at 5 Years of Age, for 7 years—That when he was about 10 years old, he was sent up a Chimney which had been on Fire for 48 hours: That during the time he was up the Chimney, his Master came, and found Fault with him, in so angry a Manner, as to occasion a Fright, by which Means he fell down into the Fire, and was much burnt, and crippled by it for Life.... That Boys are frequently sent up Chimneys while they are on Fire; and when a Boy at first learning is backward in going up, it is often a Practice to light Straw, and by that Means to force him up...."[2]

Other observers told similar stories about children who worked in mills, on farms, in the mines, and in other settings. The mistreatment of working children was an acknowledged fact. Although all young workers were not abused, thousands were.

WHAT IS CHILD LABOR?

The abuse and misuse of children at work is called child labor. It is work that exploits children. In every nation in all times, employers have exploited children and continue to do so. Such exploitation comes in many forms. Some employers pay low wages or no wages at all. Others force children to work excessive hours or fail to provide them with a safe, healthy working environment. If the exploitation is severe enough, permanent physical, psychological, intellectual, social, and moral damage—even death—can result. The work of the young English chimney sweeps was child labor.

Today no society anywhere in the world advocates child labor. Indeed most nations have laws outlawing it. Yet child labor continues and, according to a United Nations report, is a growing evil.[3] True, children don't sweep chimneys anymore, but they do work at many other, sometimes more dangerous, unhealthy jobs.

Youth employment as opposed to child labor is the employment of children at appropriate jobs with considerate employers, under healthy conditions and at fair wages. Such employment is, at least theoretically, a mutually beneficial relationship between an adult employer and a young employee. Although most people agree that child labor is wrong and youth employment has merit, many people do not agree on the distinction between the two. What one person calls child labor, another calls youth employment.

THE BEGINNINGS OF CHILD LABOR

From the beginning of civilization, children have worked. They have done tasks as family members to contribute to the household unit. Such work was part of their upbringing and a preparation for adulthood. From ancient times on, the chores—whether caring for crops, animals, younger family members, or the home itself, or participating in family handicrafts—may have been hard but probably were not harmful and may even have been fun.

During the Middle Ages, from about 476 to the late 1400s in some societies, parents believed that they *owned* their children and therefore treated them like property. Rich and poor parents alike used their children for economic gain. For example, among the wealthy an arranged marriage might increase the status, wealth, and power of a family. Kings arranged marriages of their sons and daughters in order to unite kingdoms. Among the poor, parents needing money might choose to sell or apprentice one or more of their children to keep the rest of the family from starving. An apprentice is a person required to serve another while learning a trade. Under this arrangement the parent received a cash payment for the child; the child received food, housing, and clothing; and the master received the fruits of the child's labors. The agreement between the master and the parent determined the number of years the child remained an apprentice. In any of these property arrangements the child was expected to do as he or she was told. If the child was lucky, the master was a kind one or the spouse a wise choice—but there were no guarantees.

The working child, whether apprenticed or sold, was in a vulnerable position, for whether the master was kind or cruel, the child had to work not under the supervision of a parent but under the rule of a stranger. The master alone determined the hours and the conditions, so the hours were usually long and the work hard. Children and adults alike generally accepted their lot in life, and everyone expected children of the poor to work.

THE INDUSTRIAL REVOLUTION

Three hundred years later, in eighteenth-century England, new discoveries in science and technology initiated a major trend that would change the face of society forever: replacing some human power with energy derived from sources like water and coal; and using new machines to do what humans had done in the past. Thus began the Industrial Revolution.

Coal was used to fire blast furnaces and forges, shops where iron is heated and shaped. With the increased use of coal and the production of iron, it became possible to

*One of these little Scottish coal workers has
just lost her sack of coal.*

build and power machinery. The inventions during the Industrial Revolution transformed the world from a peasant society to an industrial one, and in this new society child labor was used extensively.

The first industry to become industrialized was the textile industry. Textiles are woven fabrics such as wool, cotton, silk, and flax. Textiles are made in a complex process, starting with the production of thread and ending with the finished product, cloth.

The series of inventions that changed the textile industry began with the flying shuttle, invented by John Kay in 1733. A shuttle is an instrument used by weavers to pass the threads of the woof between the threads of the warp. Woven fabrics require both warp and woof threads. The warp is the threads set up on the loom as the first step of weaving. The woof is the threads the weaver adds to complete the fabric. The flying shuttle enabled material to be made much faster than ever before.

The next invention was the spinning jenny, which was invented in 1764 and patented by James Hargreaves in 1770. The spinning jenny replaced the spinning wheel, and for the first time weavers were able to produce more than one thread at a time. The invention of powered looms, also called weaving machines, soon followed. With these inventions textile production increased dramatically, and it was not long before factory-made cloth replaced homemade cloth.

Other inventions increased the use and production of iron and steel, which in turn quickly affected transportation and commerce. Coal-powered steam engines provided the energy for the new machinery. Each new invention inspired other inventions, and together they changed the way people lived, worked, and did business. As a result of the Industrial Revolution the major workplace shifted from the farm and home to the factory.

England quickly became the industrial leader of the world. Entrepreneurs with money to invest began building factories to house the new machinery. This construction boom required some workers to build the factories and others to work in them. The growth of manufacturing shifted to concentration of great wealth in the hands of the few.

As the number of factories grew, so did the number of people required to tend them. A labor shortage resulted, and employers turned to children. Since children, especially the children of the poor, were abundant and replaceable—if one child died, he or she could easily be replaced by another—conditions were ripe for exploitation. Employers went to workhouses, collected children, then transported them in crowds, sometimes for many hundreds of miles, to work all day and "often during the whole night" in factories.[4] A workhouse was a prisonlike home in which children and adults lived and worked when they had no other means of supporting themselves.

At first the general population believed that employing children was beneficial to both the child and the community. Work kept youngsters out of trouble, gave them early self-reliance, and provided extra money for their families. However, employing children created new family hardships because as more and more children went to work, unemployment *grew* among the heads of households. Employers replaced adults with children since children could be hired for less money. As unemployment among adults grew, families began starving. In turn, more children began working, and so the cycle continued and enlarged. The earnings of children simultaneously helped and hurt families. Naturally, it was the children of the poor who suffered. The children of the rich did not have to work in factories.

The average age at which children went to work was very young. It was not uncommon in the 1700s and 1800s for seven-year-olds to work in mills and mines. They worked eighteen hours or more a day and grew up illiterate because they did not go to school. Their parents encouraged them to work and even found jobs for them, because the choice was to work or starve. Because of child labor, children were crippled by industrial accidents, became chronically ill because they lacked proper exercise and clean air, and were prone to other diseases because of improper diets. Many died.[5]

Working conditions in the mills and mines were so bad that adults in England began coming to the aid of children. In 1796 a group of physicians in Manchester became so alarmed at the declining health of children working in cotton factories that they formed a Board of Health and appealed to Parliament, the British legislature, to stop the social evils that were killing children. Dr. Thomas Percival, one of the members of the group, wrote in a report that "children and others who work in the large factories, are peculiarly disposed to be affected by the contagion of fever, . . . the close confinement, . . . [the] effects of hot or impure air, and . . . the want of the active exercise. . . . The untimely labour of the night, and the protracted labour of the day, with respect to the children, not only tends to diminish future expectations as to the general sum of life and industry, by impairing the strength and destroying the vital stamina of the rising generation, but it too often gives encouragement to idleness, extravagance and profligacy in the parents who, contrary to the order of nature, subsist by the oppression of their offspring."[6] Dr. Percival, then, blamed not only the employers for the harsh life of children, but also the parents.

Around 1800 a growing number of enlightened people in England began speaking out against the injustice of child labor. In 1802, Parliament passed the first law regulating child labor. However, the law was not enforced and applied only to children dependent upon charity. In the following decades famous authors like Elizabeth Barrett Browning and Charles Dickens used their pens to bring the problem to the attention of the public. It was hard for the middle class and the affluent to believe the effect industrialization was having upon children.

In 1833 Parliament passed stronger measures to pro-

Getting whipped was common in mills and factories in the eighteenth and nineteenth centuries.

This British factory is being visited by a government inspector.

tect children. Although these laws helped, they were not enough. Charles Dickens once again explored the problem, this time in *Oliver Twist,* the story of a poor orphan boy drawn into the criminal world of London. Dickens pointed out the greed, cruelty, and selfishness of adults and their effect upon young children pushed too young into the work force.

It was common at the time for factories to have whipping rooms for children who misbehaved, worked too slowly, or fell asleep during working hours. It was not unusual for employers to chain children to equipment so they could not run away.[7] As bad as these working conditions were, what shocked the public more than anything else was the revelation in 1842 of the barbaric working conditions in the coal mines. Examiners found children "chained, belted, harnessed like dogs in a go-cart, black, saturated with wet, and more than half naked—crawling upon their hands and feet, and dragging their heavy loads behind them—[the children] . . . present an appearance indescribably disgusting and unnatural."[8]

When the information reached the more well-to-do public, they were outraged and pressured the government to pass laws protecting working children. However, not until the end of the nineteenth century, when economic and social conditions changed in the United Kingdom as a whole, did life improve for the working children.

T W O

AMERICA'S
CHILDREN
AT WORK

*We must learn while we are children, how to
do hard things. . . . But when you do the same
thing twenty times, a hundred times a day, it is
so dull.*
—*Lucy Larcom, an eleven-year-old New
England mill girl, 1875[1]*

The United States and the United Kingdom share a common history. Since colonial days Americans have both
adopted and adapted many of the British laws and social
practices. One of these social practices was child labor.
Child labor in the colonies began, as child labor always
does, as a result of a labor shortage.

As early as 1619, in order to meet a labor shortage in
the colonies, British and American employers recruited
large numbers of poor British children to work alongside
American-born children.[2] All of these children were as
overworked and mistreated in the colonies as in England.

The textile industry in particular relied heavily on child labor. Cloth manufacturers in the colonies followed the lead of the mother country and established spinning schools for the "education of the children of the poor," especially the girls, because "girls were more docile than boys." By the time a little girl was eight, she was old enough to be employed.[3]

By the 1700s, colonists had begun to discuss the merits of child labor and believed it was *good* for children. In 1767 the governor of New York proudly wrote that "every home swarms with children who are set to spin and card."[4]

The first industry to become mechanized was the textile industry. As a result, machine-made thread, cloth, and clothing began to replace home-crafted items. Manufacturers on both sides of the Atlantic grew wealthy, but England feared the competition from its colonies and tried to limit their growth by slowing down their progress toward industrialization. The conflict over the issue of industrialization was one of the causes of the American Revolution.

After the Revolution the mother country no longer had the power to set limits on the former colonies and so industry expanded rapidly. As mechanization increased, so did the need for workers, including child workers. In 1791, fifteen years after the United States declared its independence, Alexander Hamilton wrote, "It is worthy of particular remark, that, in general, women and children are rendered more useful, and the latter more early useful, by manufacturing establishments, than they would otherwise be."[5] The children Hamilton referred to were as young as ten and worked twelve to thirteen hours a day. Corporal punishment was not unusual and was sometimes done in special whipping rooms.

For a long time the only opposition to employment of children in the United States came from visiting English and French travelers. In 1798 the Frenchman Brissot de Warville wrote, "Men congratulate themselves upon making early martyrs of these innocent creatures, for is it not a torment to these poor little beings . . . to be a whole day and almost every day of their lives employed at the same work, in an obscure and infected prison?"[6]

In 1829, an Englishwoman, Frances Wright, scolded an American audience that "in your manufacturing districts you have children worked for twelve hours a day and . . . you will soon have them as in England, *worked to death*. . . ."[7] As in England, the more the children worked, the more they depressed their parents' wages, making their employment more necessary. While some people did try to protect the children, the few laws written were, as one historian put it, "so many dead letters."[8] And so the vicious circle existing in England became established in America.

AMERICA ACCEPTS CHILD LABOR

Why did America accept child labor? For one thing, most people had little knowledge of what was going on. The government did not record national statistics on working children.[9] For another, children were treated better than in England.[10] Although the general public accepted the whipping rooms, believing that punishment kept the devil out of the child, the beatings were not as brutal as those in England.[11] Furthermore, there were no American girls dragging loaded coal wagons deep underground in coal mines.

Another reason for accepting child labor was that many people believed working children kept parents from becoming dependent upon public charity. In addition, working children kept production costs down, and this made the nation competitive abroad.

Finally, people believed that children benefited morally from their work. It was an established belief that idleness was a sin and industry a virtue. From the earliest colonial days, the long-standing belief was that work was good for children. It built character and taught responsibility and thrift. While these may indeed result from work, in fact the employer benefited far more than the employee.

For example, throughout the nineteenth century, manufacturers in Connecticut, southern and western Massachusetts, and Rhode Island commonly hired an entire family but paid only one wage, called a "family wage." In this arrangement a man, his wife, and their children worked in the same factory but the employer paid only the man. He added a bit extra to the man's usual pay for his family's help. Everyone, including the children, was encouraged—sometimes forced—to work long hours and at night. There was no time for school, and men with large, growing families were in greater demand than single men or men with small families.[12]

CHILD LABOR AND EDUCATION

Bible reading was extremely important to the citizens of early America, and was believed to encourage religious values. But in order to read the Bible, a child first had to learn to read. The major concern of early nineteenth-century liberals was not the treatment of young workers, but rather their lack of education; illiterates could not read the Bible. Reformers also argued that democracy depended upon an educated populace, and since working children could not go to school, they would not learn how to be good citizens and the democracy would suffer.

In 1813 Connecticut passed a law requiring manufacturers to provide young workers with instruction in reading, writing, and arithmetic. However, the state did not enforce the law. Even if it had, enforcement would have made little difference since school-age children were allowed to work up to eighty-four hours a week, the same as adults. A child working that many hours would have neither the time nor the energy to attend school. Legislators, however, were ambivalent—perhaps hypocritical—about whether the best interests of the nation lay in cheap child

Making shoes in mid-nineteenth-century America

labor or in educated children. This pattern was typical throughout the country in the nineteenth century. Work conflicted with school, and America seemed unsure which to limit.

In 1830 a labor union member in Philadelphia lamented that the product of work was uneducated young people. He protested that the workers in cotton factories were primarily boys and girls from six to seventeen years old who worked from daylight until dark. "In consequence of this close confinement, it renders it entirely impossible for the parents of such children to obtain for them any education or knowledge, save that of working that machine, which they are compelled to work. . . . [The children are] being brought up as ignorant as Arabs of the Desert; for we are confident that not more than one-sixth of the boys and girls employed in such factories are capable of reading or writing their own name."[13]

The superintendent of the Fall River, Massachusetts, public school system expressed that national ambivalence between the competing values of school versus work. He admitted to an investigating body of the Massachusetts legislature that the families in his district were "so poor that the town would have to aid them, if the children were taken from their work. . . . [Furthermore] their labor could not be dispensed with in the mills nor could we accommodate them in our schools."[14] Only children whose parents could support them attended school.

John Wild, a Fall River mill employee, expressed his concern to the same Massachusetts legislature. He reported that the mill owners would take child workers "at any age they can get them, if they are old enough to stand. . . . I guess the youngest is seven. There are some that's younger, but very little." Wild added that mill owners were desperate for workers and that they regularly sent their agents into schools and pressured parents to withdraw their children from school in order to work in the mills. When Wild was asked to comment on a typical child's schooling, he replied, "When he gets done in the mill, he is ready to go to bed. He has to be in the mill ten minutes before we start up, to wind spindles. Then he starts about his own work and keeps on till dinner time. Then he goes home, starts again at one and works till seven. When he's done he's tired enough to go to bed. Some days he has to clean and help scour during dinner hour. . . . Some days he has to clean spindles. Saturdays he's in all day."[15]

In 1836, Massachusetts passed a law requiring children to be in school three months each year. Other states followed with their own compulsory education laws. Nowhere, however, were the laws enforced, and children continued to work long hours. In Lowell, Massachusetts, a major textile center, witnesses reported in 1866 that "little mites of ten were on duty nearly fourteen hours a day and then did household tasks and went to evening school."[16]

CHILD LABOR, NORTH AND SOUTH

Industrialization in the United States proceeded slowly until after the Civil War, when economic conditions changed rapidly and both the North and the South greatly expanded their industry. The combination of a critical labor shortage (there were simply not enough people to run the machines) and the preference employers had for cheap labor encouraged the nation as a whole to continue accepting child labor and its evils. The old pattern gained momentum: machines replaced men, wages dropped, children went to work replacing more adults, and more parents became dependent upon their children.

In addition, a great many New England businesses moved south. Two reasons for this migration were cheap labor and fear of the passage and enforcement of strong child labor and compulsory education laws in the Northeast.[17]

Children in both the North and South worked in flour

mills, carpet plants, foundries, machine shops, shoe factories, and garment centers. Children as young as four worked in tobacco factories.[18] They endured long hours in cramped positions in glass factories. Some worked in dangerous places underground in coal mines where they rarely saw the light of day. It was not unusual for a child to fall down an elevator shaft or be mangled by a machine. There were no safety requirements and no minimum age for running machines.

In the southern states children became virtual slaves and replaced black slaves in the mills.[19] Conditions were terrible, especially in the cotton mills, where the work was dull and unhealthy. Children died from tuberculosis, chronic bronchitis, and other lung diseases as a result of working long hours in a humid, lint-filled environment. The work also maimed and killed young machine operators. The accident rate for southern mill children under sixteen years old who worked among the moving shafts, belts, and gears was twice as high as that of adults.[20]

By 1900, 25,000 children under the age of fifteen were working in southern factories. Ninety percent of these were in North and South Carolina, Georgia, and Alabama. These states had neither compulsory education laws nor child labor laws, and the illiteracy rate was three times higher than in any other state.[21]

NEW IMMIGRANTS

If working conditions were bad in the United States, they were worse in other parts of the world. In addition, there were food shortages and people were starving in places like Ireland.

Between 1881 and 1890, 5.2 million people migrated to the United States. These new immigrants entered the labor market in large numbers. They came from European farms and villages and moved into overcrowded, filthy tenements. They were poor and mostly uneducated, and few could speak English.

Tobacco workers in New York City in the 1870s

On September 19, 1874, fire struck this factory in Fall River, Massachusetts, claiming the lives of children as well as adults.

Living conditions were so crowded and people were so poor that it was not unusual for family members to share a bed and for several families to share a bathroom. Often families would rent space in their homes. This brought in a little extra money for families and individuals and kept their housing costs down. Sometimes a non-family member working a night shift would use the bed of a family member who worked the day shift. The communities in which the immigrants lived lacked adequate housing, sewers, lighting, and garbage pickup. The results of such a life were crime, the spread of disease, a future without hope, and untimely death.

Immigrant children went to work in the same factories and mills as adults, creating a surplus of workers. The new immigrants were willing to work harder for less money than the native born just in order to survive.

To make matters worse, in 1893 the nation experienced an economic depression. It hit the country more severely than any other previous similar event. The result was unprecedented misery. There were no jobs, and the social ills that had existed before—poor housing, lack of sanitation, inadequate health care, and crime—became still more pronounced. So many people were eager for work that employers who did have jobs to offer exploited workers by paying very low wages. Desperate parents encouraged their little ones to begin work early instead of going to school. Children frequently worked "off the books"; that is, employers did not keep work records, so children either would not be paid at all or would be paid for fewer hours than were actually worked.[22] This happened especially when the child worked in the same establishment as the parent.

When the depression ended in the late 1890s, industry boomed and manpower was again in short supply. Another wave of immigrants responded to fill the need and the already existing problems worsened.

The 1900 census statistics suggested the dimensions

Doing metalwork in a home sweatshop around 1890.
This photograph was taken by the great
social-activist photographer Jacob Riis.

of the misery. An immense number of children between the ages of ten and fifteen were gainfully employed— 1,750,178, or 18.2 percent of the total population of children that age. The census did not include working children under ten or those who worked "off the books" or the many children who earned money by selling merchandise on the streets, so the figures were greatly understated.

Between 1901 and 1910 an additional 8,795,000 people came to the United States. As before, the newest immigrants were poorly educated and unable to speak English, and once again the children went to work too early.

CHILDREN IN THE STREET TRADES

The newly arrived children joined other economically disadvantaged children in what were termed the "street trades." Children working the street were in a particularly defenseless position. At first neither the parents nor anyone else acknowledged that street children had a problem. Instead, these working children were the subject of romantic stories in books like Horatio Alger's *Tom the Bootblack* and *Paul the Peddler*. Alger and others pictured these young workers as confident and self-assured, as entrepreneurs on the road to great success or noble supporters of widowed mothers. The public readily accepted this idealized version of reality.[23]

In truth, street children worked long hours in the worst kinds of weather. Newsboys, or "newsies," as they were frequently called, had to rise early enough to be on the streets to sell papers at 5:00 A.M. These same children also worked evening routes until well past midnight. While the average age of a newsboy was about twelve, many started working as young as five years old. In fact, parents and bosses learned that the younger the newsy, the more papers the child was likely to sell.[24]

Boys and girls sold apples and other fruit, peanuts, flowers, coal, ice, and wood. Others collected or stole

WAIFS AND STRAYS OF A GREAT CITY.—A GROUP OF HOMELESS NEW YORK NEWSBOYS.

WHITEY.   YALLER.   KING OF BUMS.   BUMLETS.   THE SNITCHER.   KELLY THE RAKE.
       DUTCHY.   SLOBBERY JACK.   KING OF CRAPSHOOTERS.   SHEENY.   SNODDY.

Most of the boys who frequent the Newsboys Lodging Houses are waifs, pure and simple. They have never known a mother's or a father's care, and have no sense of identity. As a rule they are known by nicknames, and they generally speak of each other only by these names.

Homeless newsies in New York City in the 1890s

junk to sell. They sold door-to-door, and they sold on the streets. They worked after school, before school, and instead of school during the week, and as long as sixteen hours a day on weekends. Although by the early 1900s some states had passed protective legislation, and the laws were not enforced.[25] Street work brought illness and even death to the young workers. In some cases bad weather was to blame. Delivery boys, for example, were known to freeze to death in their wagons. Long hours of standing on hard city pavements caused orthopedic defects. Physicians reported that the conditions under which children worked caused nerve strain, tuberculosis, and chronic throat trouble.[26] Some children, especially those delivering messages for the Western Union telegraph company or other message services, came under the influence of the lowest strata of society—prostitutes, thieves, and convicted criminals.[27]

Financial pressures forced many who were in school to leave or miss class so frequently that they might as well have not been enrolled.[28] For those who attended classes, the long workdays and resulting fatigue took their toll. Teachers reported that working children fell asleep in class, were too tired to pay attention, and fell behind in their academic work.[29]

SWEATSHOPS

Working children who were not outside on the streets, were inside in factories, many of which were sweatshops. There were two kinds of sweatshops. One kind comprised small manufacturing establishments in rundown buildings where people worked under unsanitary conditions for wages that were so low that even when an entire family worked all day and into the night, they still did not earn enough money to buy food, clothing, shelter, and proper medical care. Hunger was common. Many died in fires because they were unable to escape from the locked rooms in which they labored long hours. Sweatshop employers paid the workers by the article assembled or constructed instead of by the number of hours required to complete the task. Sometimes the worker would make only the sleeves on a garment. Sometimes they would only sew buttons or assemble part of a larger object. Such work was called piecework.

The second kind of sweatshop was the home itself. Many people lived and worked in tenements—crowded apartment buildings poorly heated, inadequately ventilated, and insufficiently lit. Like the factories, they were often firetraps. Manufacturers often gave piecework to women and children to do at home, turning the home into a sweatshop. While home industry in the form of craft work had always been a part of life, now it was different. Piecework was not creative, and the working conditions were no longer under the worker's control. A worker had to complete the work at the speed and in the manner determined by the employer.

In the early twentieth century, piecework manufacturing was an important part of the production process. The task was often simple and monotonous. It consisted of one process constantly repeated, hour after hour, day after day. The women and children who did this work were mainly immigrants. The Basso and Marachareo families who lived in New York were typical of such families. The Basso family made artificial roses on their kitchen table. They had no other place to work because they lived in only one room. "Flowers is cheap work, too cheap for anybody but us [immigrants]," said Mrs. Basso. If the whole family worked from 8:00 A.M. to 9:00 P.M. steadily, they could make 3,168 roses and earn $1.20 for their efforts.[30] In those days $1.20 would buy a simple meal for one person.

The entire Marachareo family also made flowers in their ill-lit residence. Three-year-old Angelica Marachareo worked with her mother making paper forget-me-nots.

Sewing in a home sweatshop.
Lewis Hine was the photographer.

Angelica's job was to pull the petals apart, insert the center and glue in the stem. The child could make 540 flowers a day and earn 5¢. She had to work because the family needed the nickel. "You blind yourself for thirty to forty cents a day," said Mrs. Marachareo.[31]

Many children like Angelica worked at home at a variety of tasks such as carding snaps (attaching dress fasteners to cardboard rectangles), making jewelry, sewing buttons, stringing tags, drawing threads on lace, linking and wiring beads, setting stones, and finishing underwear. Even if some children did attend school, their parents frequently kept them home to complete a work assignment.

Tenement houses were not healthy workplaces. They were firetraps and infested with vermin, often dirty, and poorly ventilated. Workers used chemicals and poisonous glue on the same surfaces on which they ate. Children easily got sick in such an environment and often communicated their diseases to others. For example, children with tuberculosis, scarlet fever, and other communicable diseases picked nuts with their teeth. They did not use nutpicks because the tool frequently broke the nut and owners would not pay workers for broken nuts.[32] Children sneezed on feather hats they made for wealthy ladies and coughed on dolls' clothes they would never play with. In this way the working poor not only suffered but contributed to contagion. Being sick, they spread disease and infection throughout the community.[33]

The latter quarter of the nineteenth century saw enormous changes in the American economy and an entrenchment and expansion of the worst practices associated with child labor. At the same time, these practices led to the beginnings of a child labor reform movement in America.

T H R E E

REFORMING
CHILD LABOR

Think of the deadly drudgery. . . . Children rise at half-past four, commanded by the ogre scream of the factory whistle; they hurry, ill fed, unkempt, unwashed, half dressed to the walls which shut out the day and which confine them amid the din and dust and merciless maze of the machines.[1]

—Julia E. Johnsen

In 1875, Henry Bergh and Elbridge Gerry, both active members of the Society for the Prevention of Cruelty to Animals, formed the Society for the Prevention of Cruelty to Children (SPCC). They were among the American philanthropists and reformers alarmed at what was happening to children, and tried to help them. At first they were interested only in the problems of child idleness and vagrancy, but as time passed they came to understand the problem of child labor.[2]

In 1884, the SPCC suggested and then drafted a regulatory factory bill for the New York State legislature. The group wanted to establish a ten-hour workday and a sixty-hour workweek for anyone under the age of twenty-one. They also wanted to bar children under fourteen from factory work. The final provision called for factory inspection so that the law would at least have a chance of enforcement.

Businesses complained that these proposed laws would make companies in New York unable to compete with those operating in states without child labor laws. Some companies threatened to move their operations elsewhere. Others said they would be forced to go out of business. Parents joined employers and agreed that it was good for children to work because the family needed the income. The SPCC was far ahead of its time. The proposal died. There was just too much opposition to it.

The organization did not give up hope but continued to press for legislation. Eventually, New York passed the Factory Act of 1886, which prohibited children under thirteen from working in factories in rural areas. However, the law was both impractical, unenforceable, and "worthless."[3] Only one inspector was assigned to oversee all factories in the state, and that inspector was required to report violations only once a year. In addition, the only proof the law required of the child's age was the child's or the parent's word. And since few factories, if any, were in rural areas, most factories were exempted.

In 1901, a few citizens in the Carolinas, Georgia, and Alabama waged active campaigns to bring about the end of child labor, and they succeeded in arousing the public to action. They also founded the Alabama Child Labor Committee, the first such organization in America. Reverend Edgar Gardner Murphy, an Episcopal minister in Montgomery, Alabama, became an early fighter in the cause. He wrote newspaper articles and pamphlets and lashed out against child labor as a moral evil. He called it economically unsound and compared the abuse to slavery. Mill owners denied the accusations, and argued that the success of the South depended upon child labor. They called the efforts to change socialism and northern interference. Murphy counterattacked and went into the mills and photographed working children.[4]

Eventually, in 1903, largely through the efforts of Murphy and his supporters, the Alabama legislature passed a law prohibiting children under twelve from working in factories. However, orphaned ten-year-olds and children who could prove that work was necessary were exempted from the law. As with earlier child legislation, there were no provisions for enforcement or inspection, and no compulsory education laws that would keep children in school and out of the workplace.[5]

THE NATIONAL CHILD LABOR COMMITTEE

All the while, other forces were fomenting. In 1904, a number of prominent citizens banded together to form the National Child Labor Committee (NCLC). The Reverend Edgar Gardner Murphy joined the group along with Alexander McKelway, an editor of a North Carolina newspaper; Owen R. Lovejoy, a minister from Michigan; James H. Kirkland, chancellor of Vanderbilt University in Tennessee; Jane Addams, a noted humanitarian; Ben B. Lindsey, a Denver juvenile-court judge; Adolph S. Ochs, publisher of the *New York Times;* Charles Eliot, president of Harvard University; and many others.[6]

Indiana senator Albert J. Beveridge was an early leader in the reform movement. He believed that private interests were making state laws ineffectual, and he urged a national solution. He introduced federal child labor legislation in 1906 but initially was unable to get support for his program, even from the NCLC.

The NCLC was a private social-action group whose goal was to survey and publicize the facts of child labor.

The organization believed that children merited a healthy and happy childhood and that if they entered the work force too young, they would be denied the opportunities that every American deserved.[7]

One of the most important decisions the NCLC made was to hire photographer Lewis W. Hine. From 1907 until 1918, he crisscrossed the country gathering data, much of it on film, about the lives of working people, especially children.

Bolstered by Hine's photographs that documented child labor practices in every state and every industry, the NCLC fought its battles one by one in the state legislatures. The NCLC hoped that if each state would change its laws, child labor would be abolished forever. In 1910, the NCLC developed a program called the Uniform Child Labor Law, which combined the best features of protective laws in Massachusetts, New York, and Illinois. These three states had some of the strongest laws on the books, even though they did not enforce them. The NCLC demanded a mini-

This is one of the Lewis Hine's earliest "photo-studies" of working children. It was taken in Corinth, Kentucky, in 1907. The original caption read: "Luther Watson of Kentucky is fourteen years old. His right arm was cut off by a veneering saw in a box factory in Cincinnati, a month ago. He was using a board to throp the belt operating the saw as there was no apparatus to do this. He is now attending school. His mother hopes to give him an education 'so's he won't have to work.'"

Poling logs was another dangerous job engaged in by children that Lewis Hine documented.

mum age of fourteen for employment in manufacturing and sixteen in mining. It urged limiting the work time for children to no more than eight hours if the child was between fourteen and sixteen. It also urged the prohibition of night work for children under sixteen. The NCLC proposal insisted on documentary proof of age rather than merely an oral statement by a parent that a child was old enough to work.[8]

The NCLC was a determined, well-organized group. It rallied the public into demanding protection and pushed state governments in the direction of passing new legislation. Between 1911 and 1913, while Hine's pictures were being circulated, thirty-nine states passed child labor laws. However, while some of the new laws strengthened existing laws and met the NCLC's goals, most legislation did not meet NCLC standards.

The NCLC was pleased with these actions but bemoaned the fact that compliance was usually voluntary. In other words, although there were laws, there were no ways to enforce them. In addition, the laws had many exemptions. The most common was the so-called poverty exemption. Under this provision, children under fourteen were allowed to work if they or their families claimed they needed the money. This encouraged abuse and undermined the laws' intent.

SOUTHERN OPPOSITION

The new child labor laws and compulsory education laws were a cause for great concern among southern mill owners in particular. These textile manufacturers feared reform efforts because they depended heavily on child labor. They employed thousands as quill boys, weavers, battery girls, clerks, doffers, sweepers, spinners, bobbin boys, buttonhole makers, spoolers, and cloth inspectors in the cotton mills; as spoolers, winders, and redrawers in the yarn mills; as machinists' helpers and spinners in woolen mills; as sweepers in thread mills; and as weavers and twisters in braid factories. Children made items like underwear, shirts, curtains, umbrellas, raincoats, and pocketbooks.[9] If the law raised the minimum working age, companies would have to replace these children with older, more expensive employees, and that would reduce profits.

Mill owners gave speeches, wrote articles, and pressured state legislatures to keep children working. A familiar argument that kept reappearing was: "The dangers of child idleness are as great or greater than the dangers of child labor."[10]

One South Carolinian argued that passage of such child labor laws in his state would "discourage manufacturing in South Carolina . . . and stop twenty per cent of the machines."[11] Another argued that if such a law were passed, "the morals of the children are going to be corrupted" because they will be allowed to "loaf around the street."[12] They objected to the passage of compulsory education laws for other reasons. They feared the education of black children and worried that if the state mandated education, children would be unavailable for work. Mississippi was the last state in the union to pass a compulsory education law, which it did in 1918. It was a weak law, since it gave local communities the option of deciding how many weeks of school a child need attend.[13]

THE BATTLE TO END NIGHT WORK

The battle to end child labor was fought on many different fronts. One front was over the issue of night work. Night work was common and therefore of particular concern to reformers, especially in glass factories, where the working conditions, especially for boys, were deplorable.

Girls who worked in glass factories generally decorated and packed the finished glass, but 98 percent of the employed boys worked in the furnace rooms, where the heat ranged between 100 and 130 degrees Fahrenheit. The young workers frequently suffered from stiff necks, headaches, colds, pneumonia, rheumatism, tuberculosis, skin irritation, cuts, burns, and eye irritation. Their work required them to squat in awkward positions near hot furnaces or stand on their feet for long periods of time. They had to endure not only the intense heat, but also the bright furnace light and the dangers of broken glass. When the night shift ended at 3:00 A.M., many of the boys had no convenient way to get home. Some chose to sleep on the factory floor or in packing boxes until five or six o'clock, when the streetcars would begin operating. Others walked the long distance home.[14]

The fight to end night work in Pennsylvania and West Virginia was the reformers' longest battle. The glass manufacturers vehemently opposed the prohibition. They claimed it was cooler after dark and therefore the most economical time to run furnaces. Furthermore, they insisted that they needed to operate their furnaces twenty-four hours a day because if the furnaces cooled, reheating them would take too long. They would lose production time and become noncompetitive. They would lose contracts and inevitably go out of business.

The glass manufacturers were convincing and had so much influence that in 1909 when Pennsylvania voted to prohibit night work for children, glass factories were exempted. The exemption continued for six more years. By 1916, thirty-seven states had provisions prohibiting children from night work. West Virginia held out until 1919.

THE FIGHT FOR A BETTER EDUCATION

Side by side with those battling to end child labor were reformers who fought against other social evils. During the time the NCLC was trying to get children out of the work force, health workers were trying to improve the nation's health care and educators were trying to get children to

Glass factories used mostly young boys in the furnace rooms and worked them at night. The caption for this Hine 1908 photo-study taken in Grafton, West Virginia, reads: "Glass blower and mold boy. The boy works 4½ hours at a stretch, then rests an hour, and continues 4½ hours more in this cramped position. He works alternate weeks on the night shift."

stay in school. All of these causes were part of a political and social effort called the Progressive Movement. From time to time the causes overlapped. Gradually the fight for compulsory school attendance that had begun in the 1800s merged with the fight to end child labor. The two issues, education and humanitarianism, together became the foundation of modern child labor laws.[15]

The movement for compulsory school attendance received more support from the general community than the movement to end child labor. The sentiment of the nation was that good citizenship required an educated population and that work was good for children.[16] Reformers worked tirelessly to keep children in school more hours per day and more days per year. A side benefit of keeping children in school was that not only did fewer children work, but those who did work spent less time on the job. However, as with child labor laws, compulsory education laws were not enforced.

THE NCLC SHIFTS TACTICS

One problem that reformers saw was that state child labor laws were not uniform. Even when there were laws prohibiting night work, the minimum age varied from age fourteen to twenty-one. There were no national standards, and no one enforced the laws.[17] After careful consideration and much debate within the organization, the NCLC decided to change its tactics and, just as Senator Beveridge had suggested ten years earlier, work toward federal legislation.

F   O   U   R

LEWIS HINE:
CHRONICLER
OF
CHILD LABOR

I have followed the procession of child workers winding through a thousand industrial communities, from the canneries of Maine to the fields of Texas. I have heard their tragic stories, watched their cramped lives and seen their fruitless struggles in the industrial game where the odds are all against them.
—Lewis Hine, 1913

Lewis Hine, whom the National Child Labor Committee hired to document the conditions of working Americans, made an enormous contribution to the fight against child labor. His photographs and reports played a key role in the work of the NCLC and made a tremendous impact on the public. Today anyone who has any doubts about the conditions under which children once labored, has only to look at the photos Hine took three quarters of a century ago. Hine did what few creative people manage to do: create images of lasting artistic *and* social value.

Lewis W. Hine was born in Oshkosh, Wisconsin, on September 26, 1874. Orphaned at age fifteen, he went to work as a laborer in a furniture factory in order to help support his mother. Eventually he went on to obtain a teaching credential and an advanced degree. His first job was as a science teacher at the Ethical Culture School in New York. He taught himself photography and used the art as a means of teaching his students to understand the world around them. In 1907, in order to earn extra money, he accepted a position as a free-lance photographer for the National Child Labor Committee. His job was to record the lives of working people.

From the time he was hired until 1918, Hine traveled thousands of miles gathering data about working conditions in the United States. He spoke to children and their parents, and everywhere he went he took pictures confirming the truth that children under the age of sixteen were working under deplorable conditions in factories, on the streets, and on farms. Not only did he take pictures of what he saw, but he also wrote and spoke about the broken lives of the suffering children.[1]

Farm and factory owners feared his presence. When Hine tried to enter factories, business executives tried to keep him out. Hine, however was determined to find the truth. To do this he often disguised himself as a surveyor, an engineer, or a bible or insurance salesman. He used whatever excuse was necessary in order to gain admission to factories. He secretly took careful notes about the children, including their age, height, and number of years working. He measured the distance between the buttons on his vest so that he could accurately tell the height of the child.

IN THE MINES

Around 1907, Hine began traveling in the anthracite region of Pennsylvania. He was a gentle man and a likable

*Lewis W. Hine, the great social-activist
photographer, at work*

person and so was able to get children to talk to him about their six-day workweek and twelve-to-fourteen-hour workday, their injured hands and aching backs, and their fear of ending their lives like their comrades—crushed or smothered to death by coal. He recorded the tedious work children did, their boredom, and their loneliness, and how "they get tired and sick because they have to breathe coal dust instead of good, pure air."[2]

Hine went down into the mines and photographed young mine workers, their faces black with coal dust, harnessed like mules to wagons full of coal. One of his photographs depicted a child, Willie Bryden, sitting alone on a hard wooden bench deep within the mine in front of a closed door. Willie's job was to wait for a signal, open the door to allow a wagonload of coal to pass by, then close the door. He sat alone all day, every day, in order to keep the air from blowing through the mine and lowering the temperature. The only light in all that darkness came from a small lamp on his hat, and the only sunshine or flowers he regularly saw were the drawings he had made on the mine door.[3]

One of Hine's most famous pictures was that of a row of young boys, black with soot, sitting knee to knee on hard wooden benches bending over rapidly moving coal. The job of these so-called breaker boys was to separate coal from the stone that will not burn. The work was dangerous because a child could easily fall into the moving coal or be injured by flying coal.

Hine also photographed the children outside the mine. Some were crippled from mining accidents. All had dull, lifeless eyes, and many wore clothes that were dirty or did not fit.[4]

IN THE CANNERIES

From the mining regions of Pennsylvania, Hine traveled to the Gulf Coast. There he photographed children as young

*Young mine workers photographed by Lewis Hine.
Can you find the one boy who is smiling?*

*Hine's photos of Willie Bryden taken in Pittston,
Pennsylvania, in 1911. The original caption read:
"Willie has been a 'nipper' for four months. His mother
said Willie was only thirteen years old, but the mine
boss told his father to put Willie to work and the
squire made out a certificate saying he was sixteen.
He waits alone in the damp and the dark for a 'trip'
to come through. He was to go to the doctor for his
cough. Nearby the gas was pouring into the mine so
fast it made a great torch when the foreman lit it.
A few days later Willie was found at home, sick."*

Breaker boys had the job of separating coal from the unburnable stone. They sat on the benches, bent over the coal, which was moving rapidly past them on belts. The work was dangerous because a child could easily fall into the moving coal or be injured by flying coal. The original caption for this January 1911 Lewis Hine photo-study, made in South Pittson, Pennsylvania, read: "Noon hour in the coal breaker. Many of the younger [emphasis added] breaker boys are not in the photograph."

The original caption for this 1908 Hine photo-study read: "This young driver has been working from 7 A.M. to 5:30 P.M. every day for a year in a West Virginia coal mine."

as four and five years old working in canneries. Some of these youngsters were the children of Polish immigrants rounded up by the seafood packagers, who promised parents healthy employment along the seashore. Instead, the packagers transported the children to work sites and then forced them to live in squalid conditions and work long hours for very little pay. Sometimes children worked with their parents either shucking oysters or picking shrimp from their shells. The shrimp gave off a corrosive chemical that made their hands bleed and skin peel and ate into their clothes and shoes. In order to stop the bleeding and harden the skin, the workers had to dip their hands into a solution of alum, a chemical substance so strong that it ate into the tins in which the shrimps were packed. "It hurts your hands pretty bad after you stay in it three days steady," said one worker.[5] Children started working as early as 4:00 A.M. and were paid by the pot, not by the hour.[6]

The illiteracy rate among Gulf Coast children was extremely high. An investigation of Texas, Louisiana, and Mississippi canneries found that among 943 working children, 11 percent of those between the ages of six and fifteen had never attended school. Forty-one percent of those between the ages of seven and thirteen should have been in school but were not. Among those children who were in school, 68 percent also worked in canneries.[7]

IN THE MILLS

Some of the most dramatic pictures Hine took were of children working in the textile mills in the Carolinas, Georgia, and New England. His pictures tended to emphasize how young the children were. Some youngsters were so little that they had to stand on boxes in order to reach the machines. He wrote about their accidents and their suffering. "Accidents happened because children were small and careless and too young for the work they were doing."[8] Unlike the coal mines, which hired only men and

In February 1911 Hine visited a cannery in the South, where he made this photo-study. The original caption read: "Little Lottie, a regular oyster shucker in an Alabama canner. She speaks no English. Note the condition of her shoes, caused by standing on the rough shells so much. This is a common sight." Below: Another Hine photo-study of oyster shuckers. How old do you think the little girl in front is?

boys, the mills also hired women and girls. Many girls worked as "spinners." The job of a spinner "was to watch rotating bobbins for breaks in the cotton. When the cotton broke the little girl had to quickly mend it and then brush the lint from the machine frame. She might tend six or eight rows of bobbins and work ten or twelve hours a day, six days a week."[9] Except for lunch she was expected to stand on her feet all those hours.

ON THE STREETS; IN THE SWEATSHOPS

In urban areas Hine took pictures of children in the street trades: wagon drivers, hawkers, messenger boys, and newsies. He captioned many of his pictures with the children's names and mention of their families. One photograph showed fourteen-year-old John Pento of Hartford, Connecticut, along with his seven-year-old twin brothers. When Hine took the picture, John already had been working seven years as a newsy. The three of them stayed on the streets selling papers every night until 8:00. Another boy, eleven-year-old Tony, also sold newspapers in Hartford, but he remained out until 11:00 P.M. because his father hit him if he didn't sell a lot of papers.[10]

Hine wrote about the physical dangers children faced from street trades and how they fell under bad influences and got involved in prostitution, crime, and narcotics. He also photographed children working in sweatshops. His photograph of a tenement sweatshop in Newark, New Jersey, for instance showed youngsters stringing milk tags. In

In August 1910 Hine photographed this "anaemic little spinner in a New England cotton mill."

"One of the many young newsboys selling late at
night (1:30 A.M.) in Jersey City (New Jersey).
He is taking a nap on the subway steps. He and
others sleep in the car barn there winter nights."
Photo-study and caption by Hine

*Hine documented this home sweatshop in New York City
at 4:00 P.M. in December 1911. The caption read:
"This ten-year-old girl is cracking nuts with her
teeth. The mother had just been doing the same. Such
conditions led to a prohibition of the manufacture
of food in tenement homes in New York State."*

his comment Hine reminded his viewers that the children worked instead of going to school.[11]

ON THE FARM

Hine discovered that child labor was as prevalent in rural life as it was in urban life. For example, when he visited the sugar beet fields in Colorado and Wisconsin, he found children doing the dangerous work of topping beets. "Topping required holding a beet against the knee and cutting off the top with a 16-inch knife that had a sharp prong on the end," Hine wrote. "All too often a child accidentally hooked himself in the leg with the knife."[12]

He wrote that some of the toppers were as young as seven and worked from 6:00 A.M. until 6:00 P.M. with an hour off at noon. He talked to Henry on a sugar beet farm near Fond du Lac, Wisconsin. Henry was "a six year old beet worker and all around slave with a tenant family."[13] A tenant farmer is a farmer who rents farmland rather than owns it.

Hine found that rural life for the children of poor tenant farmers was unhealthy, arduous, and dangerous. With pictures and words he told the American public that the agricultural work children did was not only unsuitable for their age but also inhumane. He wrote about the back pain that comes from stoop labor as a result of the prolonged bending required of those who harvest and plant. Hine recorded it all and did his best to convince people that child labor on farms must stop.

SHOCKING THE PUBLIC

Hine's pictures and essays were published all over the United States. He wrote reports and essays about them, gave lectures and slide shows, and helped design posters that advocated change. The NCLC published his findings in magazines, newsletters, pamphlets, and newspapers

*Says the caption for this Hine photo-study:
"A ten-year-old boy 'topping' beets. The
sinister-looking knife used for topping has
a hook on one end which is used for picking
up the beets. The schools do not count as
'absent' children who are out for beet work."*

Above: *Said Hine in the caption for this September 1913
photo-study made in Bells, Texas: "In the cotton
fields of this farm children as young as four or five
years old are picking cotton. A large proportion of
all the cotton is said to be picked by children
under fourteen. The very young children like to pick
at first, but before long they detest it. The sun
is hot, the hours long, and the bags heavy."*
Right: *A poster made by Lewis Hine*

WHY THIS DOUBLE STANDARD?

One New England Corporation Owns Cotton Mills In Georgia and Massachusetts.

In Massachusetts They Employ	In Georgia They Employ

Immigrant Children 16 years old and upward 10 Hours a Day.	Native Children 10 years old and upward 11 Hours a Day.

Why these Better Conditions in Massachusetts? Public Opinion Demands Them. *Why these Bad Conditions in Georgia? Public Opinion Permits Them.*

What a Reflection On

and distributed them across the nation at public meetings, state fairs, and other places where people gathered, and people were horrified at what they saw.

Hine's pictures revealed the truth and shocked the public. He felt the pain and hopelessness of the children and wanted to end the cycle of poverty that passed from generation to generation. He and the NCLC were committed to the idea that in an industrial society an uneducated child would remain poor forever.[14] Together they wanted to move people to action, to abolish child labor.

F I V E

A FEDERAL
SOLUTION
TO A
NATIONAL
PROBLEM

[The constitutional amendment is] a communistic effort to nationalize children, making them primarily responsible to the government instead of to their parents. It strikes at the home. It appears to be a definite positive plan to destroy the Republic and substitute a social democracy.
—Clarence E. Martin, President, American Bar Association, 1933[1]

Lewis Hine and the National Child Labor Committee opened the eyes of Americans to the serious social and economic problems of child labor. However, even after the public understood the situation and demanded change, little progress was made. Reformers believed that change would not come voluntarily and therefore began urging state governments to: (1) enforce a minimum age below which children could not work; (2) provide children with a minimum education before allowing them to enter the work force; (3) limit the maximum number of hours children could work; and (4) protect children from dangerous and unhealthy working conditions.

The business community would not acknowledge that a serious problem existed. Despite Hine's documentary photography and the mounting publicity of NCLC workers, business vigorously opposed reformers and said that NCLC goals would diminish production and limit national prosperity. A long battle between these two opposing points of view ensued.

One of the weaknesses of the reform movement was conflict among reformers themselves. Indiana senator Beveridge, an early reformer, wanted federal legislation, but the NCLC preferred state legislation. The American Federation of Labor (AFL)—the major representative of organized labor—and some members of the NCLC (especially those from the South) feared any sort of federal interference. The AFL wanted to keep children out of work for selfish reasons, believing that if children did not work, adult wages would rise. The AFL was not interested in working with a group whose goals seemed only child-oriented and humanitarian. Neither the AFL nor the NCLC saw reasons to cooperate and work toward a common goal.[2]

In 1912, President Woodrow Wilson declared that federal child labor regulations were illegal. A number of legislators, such as Senators Ira Copley of Illinois and William Kenyon of Iowa and Representative Miles Poindexter of Washington, thought otherwise and together prepared a federal child labor bill. However, it was not until 1916 that Congress passed its first child labor law. This law made it illegal to employ children under the age of sixteen in mines and quarries and children under the age of fourteen in mills, canneries, and factories. Children were limited to working six days a week and couldn't work past 7:00 P.M. Only businesses engaged in interstate and foreign commerce were subject to the law.

SUPREME COURT DECISIONS

Despite widespread public sentiment in favor of the legislation, the business community—especially owners of factories and mills in the South—fought it successfully in the courts. In 1918, the Supreme Court, in a 5–4 decision, declared the statute unconstitutional.[3] Congress could not extend its power to regulate interstate commerce to include issues dealing with child labor.

Congress tried again. This time it attached a child labor bill to a revenue act. It provided a 10 percent tax on the net profits from mines and factories which employed children. The bill reduced the number of working hours, raised the minimum working age to fourteen for most occupations and sixteen for night work or work in mines, and required documentary proof of age. The law remained in effect from 1919 to 1922. The result was that child labor decreased 50 percent.[4] However, a million children between the ages of ten and fifteen—one of every twelve—still labored long hours in unsafe environments.[5]

For a second time the business community—especially those with southern interests—opposed the new law, and in 1922 the United States Supreme Court declared this law, too, unconstitutional. The Court ruled that it was unlawful to regulate child labor through the use of a taxing device, adding that such an extension of the right to tax would give Congress too much power.[6] Almost immediately the number of employed children increased, as did the number of hours they worked.[7]

THE FIGHT TO AMEND
THE CONSTITUTION

After this Supreme Court decision a movement grew to end child labor by amending the U.S. Constitution. Significant organizations endorsed the proposed amendment, including the NCLC, National Educational Association, Democratic National Committee, Republican National

Committee, American Federation of Labor, National League of Women Voters, National Council of Jewish Women, National Council of Catholic Women, and National Women's Christian Temperance Union. Equally powerful forces opposed amending the constitution, including the National Association of Manufacturers, the Pennsylvania Manufacturers Association, the cotton and textile interests of North and South Carolina, the Sentinels of the Republic, Farmers' States' Rights, and the American Farm Bureau Federation.[8]

Both sides fought powerful campaigns and flooded the country with articles, editorials, speeches, advertising, leaflets, and radio broadcasts. Leaflets demanded the sovereign rights of the states and played on the fear that if the law were passed, the federal government would dictate how and when a child could work. Some even said the law would make it illegal for children to do household chores.[9] Some called the amendment a communist plot.[10]

THE GREAT DEPRESSION

While people were fighting over the child labor issue, the Great Depression began. The crash of 1929 and its aftermath had an adverse effect on the liberal cause. The country was pulled in two directions at the same time. On the one hand the Depression shocked the public into an awareness of many social problems, including the relationship between adult unemployment and child labor. On the other, as adult wages plummeted, child labor flourished. By 1933 slightly more than half the states had adopted the NCLC standards and half had ratified the constitutional amendment—passage required approval of three quarters of the states.

To get the country out of the Depression, Congress passed the National Industrial Recovery Act in 1933 and established the administration to enforce its provisions, called the NRA. The Act established a Code of Fair Competition and, in its concern over child labor, established sixteen as the minimum age for most work but eighteen as the minimum in mining and logging. Prior to this, in most states children could begin working anywhere at age fourteen. As a result, industry lost 150,000 children in mining and logging. Overall the number of employed children decreased 72 percent.[11]

The administration was so proud of this Code that in January 1934 President Franklin D. Roosevelt declared "child labor is abolished."[12] He was wrong. The Code was temporary, and many interest groups continued to oppose its provisions.

Meanwhile the fight for the passage of the constitutional amendment continued, and more people joined the cause on one side or the other. The Non-Partisan Committee for the Ratification of the Child Labor Amendment, whose membership included prominent lawyers, clergy, educators, and civic leaders, were opposed by a group calling itself the National Committee for the Protection of Child, Family, School, and Church. This latter group received support from big business and most of the American press. The press feared the amendment would prohibit children under eighteen from selling and delivering newspapers.[13]

In 1935 the Supreme Court ruled the NIRA unconstitutional and all its acts null and void. The decision was unanimous. Congress, the justices said, had not only improperly given power to the president but had also unlawfully regulated *intra*state commerce.

Within one year the number of working children increased 150 percent.[14] Reformers hoped that the constitutional amendment would bring the necessary changes, and they were encouraged when in 1936 former president Herbert Hoover made a public statement urging support of the amendment.

Yet despite his appeal and a Gallup poll that showed 76 percent of Americans in favor of the amendment, state legislatures voted against it. When the New York State Assembly defeated the proposal, despite the fact that it had the support of 83 percent of New York residents, the amendment was doomed.[15]

THE FAIR LABOR STANDARDS ACT

In June 1938, Congress passed the Fair Labor Standards Act, or FLSA. Like the Code, the FLSA made it illegal to employ children under the age of sixteen while school was in session. The FLSA was denounced by the Cotton Textile Institute and the National Association of Manufacturers, which called it a communist plot and a Nazi scheme. These organizations and others fought it all the way to the Supreme Court. The case reached the Court in 1941. By then President Roosevelt had, through his judicial appointments, changed the balance of power on the Supreme Court. The judges upheld the legality of the FLSA and gave Congress the power to protect children employed in industry and trade that engaged in international or interstate commerce.

Under the Fair Labor Standards Act, children fourteen and fifteen years old were permitted to work, but only if their work did not interfere with their schooling or health. It prohibited anyone under eighteen from working in mining, manufacturing, logging, and other dangerous occupations. The law also had a minimum wage provision that applied equally to adults and children. Finally, the law limited the number of hours per day a child could work. The overall effect of the law was to make it no longer profitable for an employer to substitute a child for an adult worker.

The FLSA had a number of weaknesses. It did not apply to children who worked on farms; sold newspapers; or worked in restaurants, retail stores, beauty shops, or laundries, among other places. Nor did it apply to children who worked for companies that did business within only one state. In actual fact, the law protected only about 25 percent of working children.[16]

The combination of public disinterest and especially farm lobby pressure combined to keep farm laborers from the protection of the FLSA. The disinterest resulted from the public's assumption that, in general, work was good for children and farm labor in particular was healthy work in the sunshine among the birds, flowers, and sweet-smelling fields. The public also believed that farming was morally uplifting and that children who engaged in it did so under the care and supervision of their parents on the family farm.[17]

The reality of farm work, like the reality of chimney sweeping, was not romantic. As Lewis Hine and others had shown, farm work was often dangerous and un-healthy. The work was physically exhausting and perma-nently damaging to children as well as adults. Illness, disease, malnutrition, anemia, wasting of muscles, poor resistance to infection, skin infections, intestinal worms, draining ears, upper respiratory infections and diarrhea were common maladies among working farm children.[18]

Farms were "factories without roofs" where children labored as paid and sometimes unpaid employees. Some people believed that farm labor was the most serious child labor problem in America.[19]

By 1940, the census figures showed a drop of nearly 41 percent in the number of working fourteen- to fifteen-year-olds and 30 percent in the number of working six-teen- to seventeen-year-olds. This figure, however, was not entirely accurate, since it included only those chil-dren working at the time of the 1930 census and not those "usually" employed but absent or temporarily un-employed on census day. Nor did it include working farm children or illegally employed ten- to thirteen-year-olds.[20] Still, the decrease in the number of working chil-dren was significant as was the corresponding increase in the number of children attending school. Clearly progress had been made.

WARTIME

When the United States entered World War II in 1941, the drain on the work force by the military led to an acute manpower shortage. To help maintain crucial domestic and military production, children again went to work in large numbers. Once again school enrollment declined, and the number of legal and illegal working children increased. The public considered work a citizen's patriotic duty, no matter who the citizen was.

This time working conditions were generally better. The combination of the war, the law, new technology, and an improved economy had eliminated sweatshop conditions and the old tenement-style employment. The youngest children rarely worked, and most elementary school children attended school. In addition children did much less arduous labor than before. No children worked in munitions plants, coal mines, or glass factories.

While one kind of child labor ended, however, another kind began. Older children began working in offices, stores, restaurants, laundries, bowling alleys, and garages, the very areas not specifically excluded in the Fair Labor Standards Act.[21]

Some old social problems were renewed. Many communities, for example, became alarmed at the number of high school dropouts. Cities like Detroit, Los Angeles, Minneapolis, Oakland, Philadelphia, and Tulsa met the problem creatively. They set up work-study programs that enabled high school students to remain in school and receive credit for on-the-job training.

Investigators found that work-study projects supervised by school personnel helped to keep teenagers in school.[22] However, when the work was not part of a formal school program, frequently employers were able to exploit the teens and preteens by having them work off the books (so there would be no record of their employment), by requiring them to do tasks which the law forbade, or by insisting that they work longer hours than the law allowed.

During the war, the federal government formed numerous committees to oversee the war effort. Under the newly formed War Manpower Commission and with the cooperation of the NCLC and the Commission on Children in Wartime, federal agencies relaxed the standards established by the Fair Labor Standards Act as it applied to teenagers. For example, fourteen- and fifteen-year-old students were now permitted to work until 10:00 P.M. if they sold fruits and vegetables and until 8:00 P.M. if they packed shrimp. In addition, the government now permitted eighteen-year-olds to work in areas it previously considered too dangerous.[23]

By 1944, the number of working teenagers had tripled and of those attending school had declined. One million fewer students attended high school than in 1940, and illegal employment had increased four- to fivefold.[24] In intrastate industry, fourteen became the permissible age for full-time work in all but fourteen states, and ten states allowed a child of *any* age to work part-time in nonmanufacturing jobs. Thirty-nine states permitted students to work after school at full-time jobs.

During the war, as in earlier times, the definition of child labor seemed flexible, and thus the cycle of tightening and loosening rules continued. After the war, the cycle continued, and it continues today as people debate the nature of child labor and whether the laws are too strict.

PEACE AND ITS AFTERMATH

World War II ended in 1945, and business began to boom, especially in the service industries and retail stores. Women and children who had started to work during the war continued working, and still more joined the work force. Many jobs were available, especially in such labor-intensive occupations as the service trades, street trades, and retailing. These very areas that were federally unregulated employed three out of every four working teens.[25]

By 1955, 16 million teenagers between the ages of thirteen and nineteen were working. Ten years later that figure jumped to 24 million. By 1975, 30 million teenagers were employed and the number was climbing. During these years, the modified Fair Labor Standards Act continued protecting the nation's youngest children against the abuses reformers had identified in the previous century. Times had changed, however, and new hazards threatened the health and safety of American workers. The risks came from toxic chemicals and the unsafe use of machinery.

In 1970, in an effort to protect workers in areas not covered by the Fair Labor Standards Act, Congress passed the Occupational Safety and Health Act and set up the Occupational Safety and Health Administration (OSHA) to enforce it. It was OSHA's responsibility to inspect the nation's workplaces and make certain that businesses obeyed health and safety regulations. Between 1970 and 1980 OSHA rigorously enforced the regulations and fined the offenders. Pilots, for example, were no longer allowed to spray pesticides over fields in which pickers were working; great caution had to be used when employees used toxic chemicals; and children were forbidden to use power-driven equipment.

Beginning in 1981, President Ronald Reagan's administration began cutting the OSHA budget, weakening enforcement. By 1988, OSHA was receiving 50 percent less funding than it had ten years earlier. As a result, violations increased. According to provisional data provided by the United States Department of Labor, detected child labor violations increased 150 percent between 1983 and 1989, and many working children were getting hurt. Numerous underage children were engaging in forbidden work activities like demolition, wrecking, and logging. Others worked schedules that exceeded the hour limitations set by the FLSA. In addition many children were working without a work permit, a document certifying that the child is healthy and old enough to do the required work.

The 1988 records show, for example, that in Atlanta, Georgia, a seventeen-year-old was killed while working as a logger; in Indianapolis, Indiana, another seventeen-year-old boy was killed while unloading sewer pipes; and in Virginia a fifteen-year-old boy died from multiple injuries when he fell off the roof he was tarring. All of these children were engaged in illegal work, and their employers were found guilty of using child labor and fined.[26]

In recent years the federal government has done a great deal to bring an end to child labor and improve the lives of working children. Child labor as it once was, no longer exists. The worst problems have been corrected. However, although most elementary-age children are in school and not at work, laws that control the number of hours and the working conditions under which the young labor are not always enforced. Children continue to work as they always have: on farms, on streets, in small businesses, or in any place they can find jobs. They work legally and illegally. Most recently, children have increasingly been working in the fast-food industry, chain restaurants, and stores. These are also the workplaces in which investigators find the most violations. Where there is a violation, there is a modern form of child labor.

S I X

CHILD LABOR
TODAY:
IN CITIES
AND TOWNS

There is not only lack of adequate information and outreach to young people, parents, employers, educators and concerned organizations about the fact that children are routinely exploited in the labor market, but there is also little information on the kind of regulations that exist to protect them.
— *Child Labor Coalition, 1991*

Today child labor is defined as the *illegal* employment of children—when the children are under the legal minimum age; when they work longer hours than allowed by law; when their compensation is unfair, illegal, or nonexistent; or when the working conditions endanger their health. As in the past, child protection laws vary from state to state, but the Fair Labor Standards Act sets a minimum standard (Bulletin 101, entitled *Child Labor Requirements in Nonagricultural Occupations* may be obtained from the

U.S. Department of Labor, Employment Standards Administration, Wage and Hour Division. You might call your senator or representative for the exact address.) When state laws are stricter than federal laws, employers must obey state laws.

The federal regulations are very specific. For example, the law states that children between fourteen and sixteen years of age may not work more than forty hours in any one week when school is not in session or more than eighteen hours in any one week when school is in session. Furthermore, children may not work more than eight hours in any one day when school is not in session, nor more than three hours in any one day when school is in session. In addition children may not begin work before 7:00 A.M. or work after 7:00 P.M. except during summer vacation, when they may work until 9:00 P.M.

Sixteen- and seventeen-year-olds may work at any time for unlimited hours in all jobs not declared hazardous by the Secretary of Labor. State laws, however, are far more restrictive.

Such are some of the conditions set forth to deal with the complexities of the working lives of children.

TODAY'S WORKING CHILDREN

Today there are two main groups of working children: the children of the poor and the children of the middle class. (Rich children may work too, but they constitute a smaller group than the middle class.) Children are motivated to work for the same reasons adults work, and when given the opportunity most American teenagers, like adults, choose to work. Two thirds of graduating high school seniors will have worked at some time during their teen years.[1]

The racial and ethnic imbalance between children who work and those who do not, mirrors the imbalance among the full-time adult labor force. That is, white children are more likely to have jobs than black or Hispanic students although black and Hispanic families tend to be poorer on average than white families. Like adult employment rates, teen employment figures are the lowest for the poorest teenagers.[2]

Among the poorest working children are recent immigrants from Asia, Mexico, and Latin America. Many of these children cannot speak English, and their parents are illiterate in any language. Many of these teens labor in sweatshops under conditions similar to those of the earlier European immigrant children. As in earlier times, these children are often too young to work, but their families are so poor that they must. Many of them show little desire to attend school and are frequently truant.

The second group of working children are from the middle class. They are the majority of the working teens. They work for their own material gain, motivated by materialism and consumerism, not poverty. They work not to eat but to have spending money and buy themselves luxuries like stylish clothes, cars, and electronic equipment. A few save money for college, and a few help their parents in the family business.[3] Among these teenagers the amount of time they work is unrelated to family income, parental education, or parental occupation.[4]

STREET WORK

Children still sell newspapers before and after school and on weekends. They usually do this in their own neighborhood. American society has accepted such work as a valuable experience despite the hours (early morning) and risks (muggings, bike injuries, bad weather, etc.). Newspaper employers hire paper boys and girls because few adults are willing to work at the pay rate the newspapers offer. Some newspapers offer scholarships or bonuses to their young employees.

Candy selling is another street trade that involves children. While selling candy can be a legitimate job for children (numerous nonprofit organizations have children selling candy as a fund raiser), some employers are less than honest. For example, a fast-talking crew boss may lure children into the operation with promises of big money and convince the children's parents that some of the money earned will go toward charity. Often it never does, and the children may receive as little as $1 for every $5 box of candy sold. If they sell nothing, they earn nothing, no matter how many hours they work. Some of these companies are nothing more than rackets. Their phone numbers cannot be traced, they have no business address, and they pay no taxes.

In Washington, D.C., investigators found children working twenty, thirty, even forty hours a week selling candy door-to-door. Some of these children were under fourteen.[5] In other parts of the Northeast, where this candy scam is common, children are driven from neighborhood to neighborhood in large vans and must continue to work until the boss drives them home. Children often work as late as 11:00 P.M. It is illegal for children under age sixteen to work past 7:00 P.M. on school nights or to work more than eighteen hours per week. In one New Jersey city, parents filed assault charges against their daughter's crew boss.[6] Federal investigators have jurisdiction in these candy scams only if the crew boss crosses the state line with the children and the company's annual sales exceed $250,000.

SWEATSHOPS

Children still work in sweatshops. A "modern" sweatshop is any business that routinely and repeatedly violates wage, hour, and child labor laws and disregards the health and safety of its employees. The Fair Labor Standards Act and later the Occupational Safety and Health Act were intended to outlaw such businesses. Yet the practice persists, particularly in the Northeast. Investigators have found children working in overcrowded rooms with poor ventilation in buildings where the stairways were in disrepair, the bathrooms unsanitary, and the fire extinguishers inoperable.[7]

Dr. Philip Landrigan, a professor of community medicine and pediatrics at Mount Sinai School of Medicine in New York, who is a physician and specialist in occupational medicine, testified before Congress in 1989 on the problems facing children in modern-day sweatshops, including company-based sites and sites where industrial homework is done. Industrial homework is work, often assembly work, that an employee does at home instead of in the employer's place of business.

Landrigan was part of a team of investigators that visited work sites throughout New York during a six-month period. Many of the sites were sweatshops. For example, investigators saw fourteen-year-olds working for low wages on dangerous machinery in belt and garment factories, although the law prohibits children below the age of eighteen from using power-driven machinery. The team also saw children as young as five passing garments between women working on sewing machines, and such children, of course, were not paid. Their mothers were paid not by the number of hours they worked but by the number of pieces they completed. Since the women could produce more when their children helped, they encouraged their children to work with them. Children sometimes stayed home from school in order to work. In one garment sweatshop, a twelve-year-old was working in an environment where the toilets malfunctioned, where the workers prepared their food next to machines that were in operation, and where at lunchtime people ate from plates on the littered workshop floor.[8]

In his testimony, Dr. Landrigan spoke of children coating wires with a thin layer of metal in rooms that had such poor ventilation that the very act of breathing sickened the children. He told about youngsters working with industrial

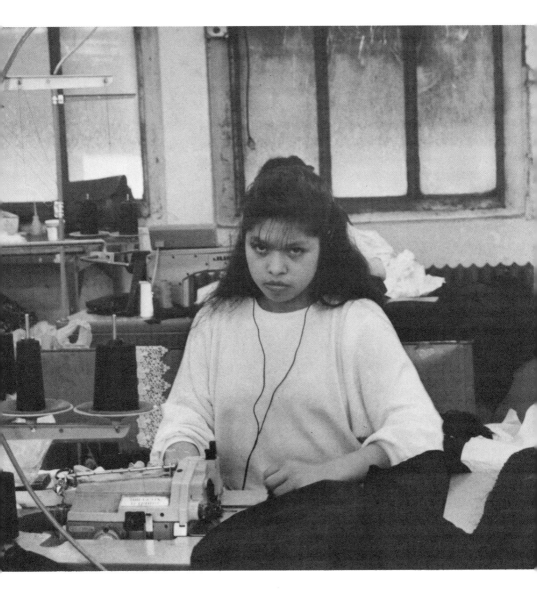

When the photo was taken in May 1990, this teenage girl was working in a garment shop in New York City. She was putting in more than eight hours a day, had no medical benefits, and received no overtime pay.

chemicals like cadmium, beryllium, and asbestos in the home assembly of jewelry. They did this work on the kitchen table, the table on which the family ate their meals. Exposure to cadmium can lead to stones in the urinary system, kidney failure, and inflamed lungs; exposure to beryllium can lead to such illnesses as lung disease and skin ulcers; and exposure to asbestos can lead to lung disease and cancer.

Landrigan referred to the many children working at home in the needle trade. They performed such tasks as sewing and pressing cloth. Some fabrics melt a little when they are exposed to heat and release formaldehyde fumes. Formaldehyde is a chemical that causes mutations (harmful changes to cells that can cause disease and lead to birth defects in offspring) and other serious problems and is so dangerous that its use has been banned in high school science laboratories. Finally, Landrigan described children being exposed to lead as they assembled auto batteries or made stained-glass windows. Lead poisoning may cause chronic pain and muscular paralysis, among other things.

Landrigan also described "chronic fatigue, blighted childhood, lost education and the perpetuation of the cycle of family poverty."[9] He concluded that the illegal employment of children and employers' failure to provide a safe and healthy environment for their employees produced many occupational diseases.

Experts agree that the number of sweatshops has been increasing in recent years. How many actually exist is not known, since it is impossible to look into every home or building to search for such activity.[10] Sweatshop employers hire children, cut adult wages, and pay no overtime, but when an investigating agent walks into a sweatshop, the news spreads quickly and the children are "squeezed out the door" before the investigator can talk to them. If the investigator asks about working children, "everyone dummies up."[11]

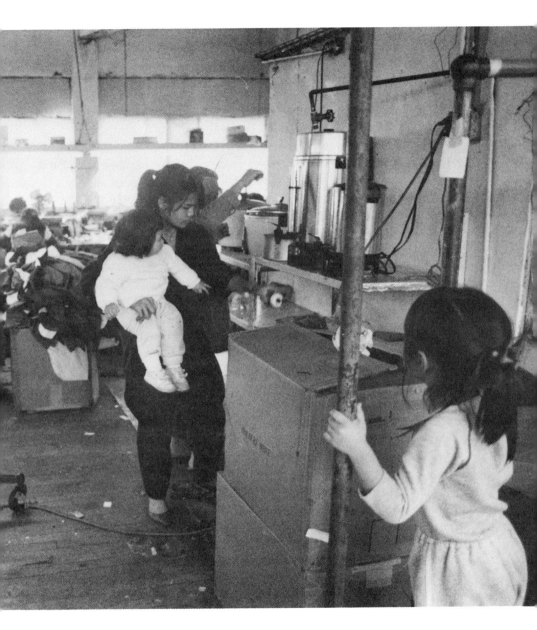

*Children still often help their mothers
in sweatshops like this one in New York City.*

SALES AND FOOD SERVICE

More youths work in sales or food service than in any other field. Nearly 50 percent of working teens work in sales and nearly 46 percent in food service. A great many teens work in stores, including grocery stores, drugstores, variety stores, clothing stores, and music stores. Anything that has been sold in a store has probably at one time or another been sold by a teenager. In addition to selling, a teenager working in a store may be asked to perform any number of other duties such as opening or closing the shop or helping with cleanup, inventory, packing and unpacking, shelving, and pricing. Working in a store is generally not dangerous, but the hours a young person works often exceed the legal restrictions.

Working in the food service industry, on the other hand, may be dangerous. Dr. Landrigan tells of two boys ages fourteen and fifteen who, within six months of each other, cut off their left hands in the same butcher shop. Dr. Landrigan has stitched up children who have gotten their fingers amputated by dough slicing machines and kneading machines in bakeries.[12] Under the FLSA it is illegal for students to operate these machines.

The General Accounting Office of the United States government surveyed the directors of state labor departments and found that in New York alone, half of the 5,000 restaurants "met the criteria for sweatshops." Fast-food restaurants routinely kept children working beyond midnight on school nights and frequently paid less than minimum wage with no overtime. In addition, restaurants often violated fire codes by blocking exit doors, overloading electric circuits, and handling combustible materials improperly.[13]

In Milwaukee, Wisconsin, Terrence Falk, a high school English and speech teacher, worried enough about his students to investigate why they were falling asleep in class and generally lagging in academic performance. He wondered what they were doing outside of school and learned

Many teens work in fast-food restaurants. The question is: Is this child labor or youth employment?

about the work schedule of several of them. For example, he found that one boy, a high school junior, worked every day until after midnight at a McDonald's and that a sophomore girl worked at a Taco Bell six days a week until at least 10:00 P.M. The academic performance of both these students had slipped. The girl's grades came down a grade and the boy was in danger of failing. A third student usually worked until 3:00 A.M. at Burger King. He often did not report to school the next day and talked occasionally about dropping out of school entirely. Falk found the same pattern repeated not only in his class but in different schools throughout the city.[14]

When children go to school tired, their grades often go down, attendance becomes spotty, and dropouts increase. Teachers then tend to lower their expectations and give less homework, because too many students fail to complete their assignments.

ACTING

Children also work in the entertainment industry. As of 1987, more than 5,000 children under the age of nineteen were members of the Screen Actors Guild. The organization is affiliated with the AFL-CIO labor union, and its purpose is to protect the interests of actors and actresses who make commercials or work in the film and television industries. The assumption is that working actors and actresses need an intermediary between themselves and their employers. People also assume that parents will not exploit their children.

In order to get just one job, a child may have to have as many as seventy auditions. Agents who help children find jobs and negotiate contracts for them tell stories about overanxious parents who "exploit their children physically, emotionally, and financially as they drive their children from one audition to the next, hoping for the big break."[15]

In California, a gathering place for child actors and actresses, the law does not require parents to set aside most of a child actor's earnings into a special savings account belonging to the child alone. On the average, only 25 percent of what a child earns is actually saved for the child's future. Child actors and actresses are sometimes placed in a position of supporting their families.

SETTING NATIONAL PRIORITIES

The FLSA and OSHA are the primary federal laws regulating wages and working conditions for all American workers, including children. Since their passage, enforcement has varied from rigorous to lax, depending upon economic conditions, national goals, and reformers' zeal to keep children safe. As a nation, we have been ambiguous about our priorities. When there is a conflict between school and work, we have difficulty agreeing what should come first. In addition, we seem unable either to provide a healthy work environment for all children or to balance work with school in a way that satisfies everyone.

S E V E N

CHILD LABOR
TODAY:
ON THE FARM

*Agriculture has come to surpass mining as the
most dangerous occupation.*
*—Drs. Susan H. Pollack, Philip J. Landrigan,
and David L. Mallino, 1990[1]*

Just as there are two main groups of working urban children, the middle class and the poor, so too are there two
groups of working farm children: those whose parents or
families own a farm or farms (mostly the middle class and
the wealthy, including corporations) and those whose parents do not. The former work on their family farm under
the supervision of their parents, while the latter work on
other people's farms as hired laborers.

Although children who work on farms owned by their
parents are seldom the victims of labor exploitation, they
nevertheless are often hurt or killed in farming accidents.
On July 10, 1989, for example, twelve-year-old Shaun
Petersen was helping his father by shoveling corn into a

machine. One of his shoelaces got caught in the moving gears, and he was pulled into the machine to his death.[2] Farm accidents such as this one happen frequently. Children who work for strangers are also accident victims, but in addition many are exploited.

Hired children may be white, black, Hispanic, or Asian. Many of them are migrant laborers. Migrant laborers move from state to state picking fruits and vegetables as they ripen. Since the workers generally do not have a permanent home, the children do not have regular access to school. The problems they face stem from the lack of education and legal protection, unsafe pesticides and machinery, and poverty. The outcome is serious accidents, poor health, and, frequently, untimely death. In the past forty years, little progress has been made to improve their working conditions.

BACKGROUND

In 1950, a presidential commission studied farm labor and found 395,000 children between the ages of ten and fifteen working on farms that did not belong to their families. Large numbers of these children were suffering from physical and mental problems caused by their farm work. Twenty years later, in 1970, the United States Department of Labor made a similar study and found similar health problems among farm workers. The major difference between the two studies was that the number of working farm children had more than doubled in twenty years. In Florida, Texas, and California, records show that "black and Chicano children begin serious work in the crops when they are between nine and twelve years old."[3] Many of these were unable to read and write and were generally in poor health. Some of the working children were as young as five and six years old.[4]

Through the years various individuals and special-interest groups have examined the farm labor problem

Although child labor has been banned on American farms, thousands of young children still work in the nation's fields. This photograph of the Sanchez family was taken in 1988 in Hollister, California.

and made reports and recommendations. Among those involved was Dr. Raymond M. Wheeler, a physician, who spent a great deal of time studying and treating the poor throughout the South. In July 1970 he presented his findings to the Senate Migrant Labor Committee. Wheeler found that the life expectancy of a farm worker was twenty years less than that of the average American; the death rate from pneumonia and flu was 200 percent higher than the national rate. Many of the children who came under his care had malformed backs caused by the prolonged stoop labor required of pickers. He also reported a serious lack of health care and the frequent loss of hearing among children because of untreated ear infections. Living conditions for children and adults, he said, were primitive.[5] There was rarely either plumbing or electricity in their homes, and sanitation facilities were almost nonexistent.

In the 1970s the American Friends Service Committee, a nonpolitical Quaker group, studied the problems of children working in agriculture in Washington State, Oregon, Ohio, Maine, and California. At the time, according to the study, an estimated 25 percent of the nation's paid labor force in agriculture were children.[6] In Washington alone, 99 percent of all migrant children over the age of six worked in the fields during the picking season.[7]

MODERN CONDITIONS

Farm children may work in groups with other children or with their parents in the hot sun or chilling rain. Picking crops is backbreaking and repetitive, and the hours are long. Children too young to pick may fetch empty containers for their parents, bring water or lunch, or haul full containers to the ends of rows. Picking is a kind of agricultural piecework. Pickers are paid by the basket they fill, not the hours they work. Adult wages are so low that children have to work in order to help support their families. Judging by the volume picked, a ten-year-old child

Left: *Alejandra Sanchez was eleven years old when this photograph was taken in 1988.*

Below: *In 1984, when this photograph was taken, Louis, age nine, had just come to the States from Haiti and was working on his first job—in a pickling-cucumber field near Salisbury, Maryland. Children under age twelve are prohibited from laboring in agriculture.*

does not pick very much; nevertheless the earnings are important.

Many farm owners would prefer not to hire children. However, some families are so desperate for money that if an owner won't permit the children to help out in the field, the family may choose another farm. Owners desperate for pickers will bend the law or look the other way and permit children to work.

ILLITERACY AND POVERTY

Picking families are mostly poor. They stay in a community only long enough to complete a harvest. Many children either do not attend school at all, or if they do, they attend irregularly and switch schools frequently. Authorities rarely enforce compulsory school attendance. Generally, the children can't keep up with their peer group, and they fall behind in their studies.

Many migrant children prefer not to go to school because they are embarrassed by the clothes they wear and the free lunches they receive. Poverty often means no magazines or books in the house, few toys, and illiterate parents. The temporary "homes" may lack electricity or a quiet place to read. For all these reasons children quit school.

Poverty means children live in shacks and sometimes old buses. They may have to share a kitchen with several families and use an outdoor privy built too close to the drinking-water supply. The children are frequently sick. Reports author Robert Taylor: "Malnutrition among migrant kids is ten times higher than the national rate; farm worker babies suffer 25 percent higher infant mortality...."[8] In 1978, the Civil Rights Commission reported that worms and parasites were common maladies in the intestines of farm children and attributed these problems to poverty and the lack of sanitation and health care.[9]

PESTICIDES AND ILLNESS

Farm children are frequently exposed to dangerous pesticides as they work. The children get the pesticides on their skin when they brush against the treated leaves and breathe the poisons in as they work. Young children ingest the poisons when they put their fingers in their mouths. Although it is illegal to spray on a field where people are working, it is not illegal to spray in the adjacent field. The wind carries pesticides from field to field, and the children inhale the poisons as they breathe.[10] Some children are born deformed because their parents were exposed to toxic pesticides.[11] Farm poisonings are a regular part of farm work. According to Linda F. Golodner, "It is commonly known that children under the age of ten are working in the fields during school hours, and are working twelve-hour days and exposed to pesticides with no access to field sanitation."[12]

Scientists have studied the effects of pesticides on adults, but similar studies have not been made to show the effects on children. Many physicians believe that an equal quantity of poison will have a worse effect on a child than on an adult. A child's body is smaller than an adult's and will react more quickly and violently to chemicals. In addition, a migrant child who grows up to be an adult farm worker will have been exposed to chemicals over a long period.

Drs. Susan H. Pollack and Philip J. Landrigan, physicians at the Mount Sinai Medical Center in New York, are engaged in an ongoing study of the health hazards of child labor. In 1990 they reported that the widespread use of

Migrant children and their families often live in squalor. This picture was taken in 1972 near Bowling Green, Ohio.

pesticides is sickening and permanently damaging the health of working farm children. They pointed out that while regulations govern the use of pesticides, these regulations are neither adequate nor enforced. There is a growing urgency, say Pollack and Landrigan, to keep better records and conduct more studies of the effects of pesticides on children. They also urge stronger laws to protect children.[13]

ACCIDENTS

Serious injury as a result of farm accidents is another problem common to farm children. In November 1974, a research team at the Mayo Clinic in Rochester, Minnesota, began keeping records of children treated at St. Mary's Hospital for farm accidents. They reported their findings in 1985. At that one hospital during that nine-year period, there were eighty-seven injured farm children younger than sixteen; fifteen had had body parts amputated by farm machinery, thirty-six had long-term disabilities; and four had nerve damage.[14] Despite the reports, the problems continued.

In September 1989, the *Wall Street Journal* on its front page reported a "farming injury epidemic" among children, with 300 deaths and 20,000 injuries annually in farm accidents.[15]

Farm accidents have many causes. One is that the children operate sophisticated farm machinery they are too small and too young to handle safely. They routinely operate drive tractors, wagons, and power takeoffs (rotating drive shafts which transfer power from a tractor to a piece of farm machinery). Another is that frequently the equipment itself is unsafe.

After the death of her eleven-year-old son, Keith, in a farming accident, Marilyn Adams founded the consumers advocacy group Farm Safety for Just Kids.[16] According to her, modern farm machinery is so unsafe that it is easy for a child to fall into a moving corn loader and suffocate. Only one manufacturer, she said, is researching the possibility of putting a grate on the machine to prevent such a fall. "Eight other makers of similar machines are satisfied to use only warning stickers," she said.[17]

LAWS

Just as in the industrial areas of the United States a half-century before, it is profitable for farm employers to hire children along with their parents. Families, out of ignorance and financial necessity, collaborate with employers to evade state laws.

Farm children are not protected by federal law, and state laws designed to protect the children are easily evaded since there are few inspectors to enforce them. In 1990, according to the United Farm Workers of America, "800,000 underage children survive by harvesting crops with their families across America."[18]

Linda Golodner, an advocate for children, calls current laws "intolerable" since "they don't protect our children."[19]

E I G H T

OPERATION
CHILD
WATCH

*Protecting our children—America's future—
from exploitation in the workplace is a funda-
mental duty of the Labor Department.
—Elizabeth H. Dole, Secretary of Labor,
March 15, 1990[1]*

In March 1990, 500 federal investigators from the United
States Department of Labor began Operation Child Watch,
a well-publicized crackdown against violators of child
labor laws. The campaign was unannounced and lasted
three days. Newspapers flashed headlines such as "Thousands of Children Doing Adults' Work" and "Burger King
Faces Charges It Violates Child Labor Laws." It is not certain why Elizabeth Dole, the secretary of labor at the time
of the sweep, chose that time to dramatize the child labor
problem. Perhaps it was because over the previous year
various newspapers had highlighted the issue. For example, a March 26, 1989, article in the *New York Times* indi-

cated that businesses were employing teenagers regularly as a way of meeting their employment needs during labor shortages.[2] On May 14, 1989, an article in the *Philadelphia Inquirer* cited an increase in child labor violations.[3] A few days later the *Washington Post* reported increased hearing loss among teenagers working around noisy farm machinery.[4] On May 18, 1989, the National Consumers League announced the start of a study of contemporary child labor issues.

Sometime during 1988 Congressman Charles E. Schumer, Democrat of New York, and Congressman Don J. Pease, Democrat of Ohio—both from highly industrialized areas—became interested in the child labor problem. In early August, Schumer asked the General Accounting Office (GAO) to study the extent of sweatshops in the United States. The investigation revealed many child labor violations. After seeing the report, Schumer requested a more in-depth study of the problem, particularly as it applied to his home state of New York. In response, in June 1989 the GAO issued a report entitled *"Sweatshops" in New York City: A Local Example of a Nationwide Problem*. This report revealed still more child labor violations. In November, Congressman Pease requested that the GAO investigate the issue of child labor throughout the United States. The information in the report was shocking and available to government officials before the publication of the document.

On February 7, 1990, William C. Brooks, Assistant Secretary in the Department of Labor, in a speech before the Child Labor Advisory Committee, publicly recognized a "serious and troubling trend" in the nation's use of child labor.[5] Everything came together the following month in the three-day sweep in which federal officers identified 11,000 illegally employed minors, one half the number detected in all of 1989 by the Department of Labor.[6] One year later the government revised the figure upward to 28,000 illegally employed minors. According to Secretary

Dole, the companies the government chose to investigate were those which "historically have been offenders."[7] The GAO's final report, "Child Labor: Increases in Detected Child Labor Violations Throughout the United States," became available in April, but once again, the findings were available to Congress and the Labor Department before the document was published.

FINDINGS

The preliminary report indicated that detected child labor violations had increased from 10,000 in 1983 to 25,000 in 1989, an increase of 150 percent in six years, and that these violations had occurred in every state and in every possible category: minimum age, maximum hours, hazardous occupations, and dangerous working conditions.[8]

Most violations involved teenagers working more hours or later hours than federal law allowed. The Labor Department estimated that nationwide 42 percent of all illegally employed minors (children under the age of eighteen) worked in restaurants and another 26 percent in grocery stores. A fraction of minors worked in strictly forbidden occupations like construction and manufacturing, or were working at jobs that involved the use of dangerous machinery like power-driven meat slicers, dough mixers, and paper bailers.[9]

The GAO report found that in 1988, 31,500 children under the age of eighteen had been injured or made sick as a result of their work and that eleven of the twenty-nine people under age eighteen killed in work-related accidents were doing illegal work like roofing and excavating, or using dangerous equipment like power-driven hoisting machines and woodworking tools. The report admitted that the statistics were incomplete and did not account for all of the unhealthy and dangerous circumstances in which children work. It was difficult for the government to make a complete report and compare the accident rate of injured children in one state with the accident rate of injured children in another state because the laws of reporting such incidents vary from state to state. California, for example, requires that employers report injuries after a person misses one day of work, but in Tennessee no accident report has to be made until an employee misses a week of work. Some states do not require any accident report on workers under the age of eighteen. In other words, there is no way to know exactly how many work-related injuries or illnesses involve minors.

Despite incomplete statistical data, the picture of injured children that does emerge is alarming. One has only to look at hospital and insurance records and listen to the words of doctors and parents to worry about the health and welfare of American children. For example, in 1986 the New York State Workers' Compensation Board awarded 1,333 children compensation for work-related injuries. Of these, 541 were for permanent disability. A Massachusetts study revealed that 24 percent of the injured children treated in hospital emergency rooms had sustained their injuries at work.[10]

Working environments in some regions of the country were far more dangerous for children than in other regions. Massachusetts, for example, had the largest number of detected illegally employed children, with Pennsylvania running a close second, followed by Missouri, New York, Florida, and Texas. No state, however, was exempt. In Georgia and Alaska, children died as a result of their illegal work in the logging industry. In Virginia and Indiana, children were killed while working on construction sites.[11]

STATE ACTION

State legislatures, alarmed at the findings of the federal government, began also to study in detail what was happening in their own states. Among the first state legislatures to study the matter and consider limits on working hours were Florida, Hawaii, Nebraska, New York, North Carolina, Ohio, and Wisconsin.

WHY THE INCREASED VIOLATIONS?

The Labor Department and GAO reports suggest several reasons for the increase in the number of child labor violations, the major one being a shortage of adult workers.[12] William C. Brooks, Assistant Secretary for employment standards in the United States Department of Labor, suggested that as "the composition of the work force changes, employers are pressured to look around for workers to fill entry-level jobs. Some employers have reacted to labor shortages by employing kids in ways that violate the FLSA."[13]

Another reason is the decline in the number of young workers. If employers cannot find enough adults or older teens to fill jobs, they will hire whomever they can, even if it means breaking the law.[14]

ENFORCEMENT

Enforcement of child labor laws has always been difficult. For one thing, the penalties have never been great enough to deter violators. For example, judges have seldom imposed the maximum fine. In 1989 the average fine for a violations involving a minor was only $165, an amount that can easily be absorbed into the cost of doing business. Recognizing this problem, the GAO report suggested that the government increase fines so that they were large enough to deter violations. Secretary Dole agreed and in addition suggested that the government changes the way it calculates fines so as to ensure a fivefold increase in the money assessed.[15]

The public and the news media were so irate at both the number and the seriousness of the violations that Congress took action and held hearings to further investigate the problem. Congressmen Tom Lantos of California joined with Schumer and Pease to introduce the Young American Workers Bill of Rights. The result was that on November 5, 1990, the Fair Labor Standards Act was changed by Congress and the maximum fine for child labor violations raised to $10,000 from the previously existing maximum of $1,000. However, for employers to be fined the government must still prove that they knowingly hired an underage child to engage in work they knew was illegal. This may be difficult to prove. Nevertheless, John R. Fraser, Acting Wage and Hour Administrator, expects that the greater the violation, the higher the fine. How large a firm is, how often a minor engages in illegal work activities, and how dangerous that activity is will help determine the size of the penalty.

Enforcement of the law is also difficult because there are only about a thousand compliance officers whose job it is to enforce the FLSA. Therefore, the Department of Labor is able to inspect only a fraction of the business establishments covered by the law. In 1989, for example, they inspected 1.5 percent of the 2.6 million workplaces. Since the department spends less than 5 percent of its time on child labor law compliance, it is no surprise that until the sweep the number of citations were few. The GAO suggested that one way to improve enforcement would be to hire more enforcement officers.

The GAO also suggested that government agencies work together to improve enforcement. For example, if the Occupational Safety and Health Administration, the Department of Labor, and state agencies cooperated and shared information, more might be able to be done to stop violations.

How would increased law enforcement be financed? One way would be to increase the cost of work permits. Another would be to use the fines for enforcement. There are objections to this latter suggestion on the grounds that it represents unappropriated funding for a federal agency. The belief is that if the agency wants more money, it should try to obtain it through the ordinary government budget process.[16]

THE
C U R R E N T
D E B A T E

*It is the AFL-CIO's position that the basic occu-
pation for all young persons should be their
education. The message should be clear that
education comes first and that work is a sec-
ondary priority.*
  *—Rudolph Oswald, Director, Department
  of Economic Research, AFL-CIO[1]*

Today, many children work, some because they have to
and others because they want to. Sometimes the work
seems harmless enough, while other times it doesn't. As in
the past, some people believe that youth employment is
beneficial and others that it is not. Sometimes the needs
and agendas of the various parties involved—children,
employers, parents, educators, reformers—are in conflict.

One aspect of the debate revolves around the percep-
tion of youth employment. There is no agreement on
where youth employment ends and child labor begins.

Some people see youth employment as benign and the abuses overstated. They would like to see rules and regulations loosened or even eliminated, and emphasize the positive: the nation's need for labor and the benefits for children. Other people view the abuses as more serious and advocate enforcing existing laws more strictly. Still others view the abuses as very serious and want to see laws strengthened and restrictions increased. These latter camps argue that all too often what starts out as acceptable youth employment ends up as child labor. These groups dwell on the negatives, most importantly, hazards and extremes.

The current debate in various quarters centers around several related questions:

- Should children work at all, even if the working conditions were to adhere to the letter of the law and the hazards were nonexistent?

- Are there violations and hazards, and are they serious? In other words, is some youth employment really child labor?

- If there are indeed violations and hazards, are they serious enough to warrant greater restrictions on youth employment?

SHOULD CHILDREN WORK EVEN UNDER IDEAL CONDITIONS?

Assuming "perfect" working conditions, there are many good reasons for children to work. Youth employment brings income to those who need it. The right kind of labor has the potential of helping young people learn how to handle money, take more responsibility, manage time, work as part of a team, and meet the obligations set by a boss. Work contributes to personal growth and self-worth. It can be a bridge between childhood and adulthood.

Work exposes teenagers to new experiences, such as putting them in contact with people they would not ordinarily meet, and helps them to learn firsthand what it's like to participate in our free-enterprise system. Youth employment may boost the economy as a whole because it encourages spending and increases the amount of money in circulation. Those who favor youth employment believe, also, that unemployed children tend to get into trouble.

On the flip side is another set of arguments criticizing youth employment as it exists today. By working, children reduce the time available to study. Learning, opponents of youth employment say, should be a child's first priority. Students who work long hours are often too tired to perform well in school. When this happens they limit their opportunities to acquire the education they will need to earn a good living in a highly technical society. Reformers argue that while business and the national economy may benefit from youth employment in the short run, in the long run the nation needs a well-educated work force. It's bad enough that students who work the legal number of hours are deviating from their main task; it's even worse for children who work over the legal maximum number of hours. In addition, studies show that working teens tend to use more drugs, alcohol, and tobacco than teens who do not work simply because the working teens have the money to do so.

Opponents of youth employment also argue that it is better for children to spend their free time doing something other than work.[2] Aren't the teen years best spent dreaming, playing, testing one's own skills, and exploring life's possibilities?[3] Ellen Greenberger, professor of social ecology at the University of California, Irvine, and Laurence Steinberg, professor of family studies at the University of Wisconsin, Madison, say in their book on teenage employment that the teen years are an important time in life for intellectual and emotional growth, a time to develop family relations and personal relationships, but that students who work have little time for this.[4]

Students, like adults, are divided on the issue. Ryan, a seventeen-year-old high school junior who works at a Burger King, speaks for many working youths when he says, "If I want to work, there should be no law against it." And Karen, a fifteen-year-old sophomore, feels that working less would not automatically mean her grades would get better. "I could study my whole life and I'd probably still never get A's."[5]

On the other hand, when Geoff was a seventeen-year-old high school senior he quit his job when his grades started to go down. He realized he needed good grades to get into a good college. "At school I was just doing the minimum to get by. I'm glad I quit. It took off the pressure and my grades went up. But when I quit, my boss really yelled at me and said it was my obligation to find a replacement." After graduating high school, going on to college, getting a degree, and landing a good job, he has decided to return to college for additional education.[6] The job market is very competitive.

ARE THERE VIOLATIONS?

Both sides agree that violations do exist. Disagreement rises over the nature of the violations.

Working Hours

Employers say that on the rare occasions when there are child labor violations, they are unintentional and are not as bad as they appear to be. They contend that "the number of alleged violations . . . are but a small fraction of the total number of minors who are lawfully employed."[7] They insist that the numbers should be taken in the context of the whole.

For example, Demoulas and Market Basket, a grocery

chain based in Tewksbury, Massachusetts, has 1,000 fourteen- and fifteen-year-olds working in its forty-three stores. According to an executive officer, William Marsden, "if every individual worked six minutes past [the legal hour], once a year, that's 1,000 violations. If you had 1,000 violations and you have forty stores, that's twenty-five violations per store. You are talking about one violation every other week." According to Marsden, the numbers may look terrible, but it's really not so bad if one looks at the entire picture.[8]

Violations, say employers, are often caused by the complexity of the laws. For example, federal law says that fourteen- and fifteen-year-olds may not work past 7:00 P.M. However, in the state of Oregon the time is moved back to 6:00 P.M., in Wisconsin they can work until 8:00 P.M., and in Texas till 9:00 P.M. Federal law requires employers to obey the law that is most restrictive, whether it is state or federal. According to a representative for the National Restaurant Association, "Many operators simply do not have the in-house resources or personnel to research all federal, state, and local laws and regulations."[9]

Some employers find it difficult to figure out what kind of work the law permits and what kind it does not. For example, the law allows fourteen- and fifteen-year-olds to perform "kitchen work and other work involved in preparing and serving food and beverages" but prohibits "cooking and baking." What fifteen-year-olds are permitted to do at lunch counters, they are not permitted to do elsewhere. In addition, different compliance officers in different regions interpret the law differently.[10]

Granted the laws are complex, but supporters of current or more restrictions greet such arguments as excuses. They believe that giant operations—for example, a McDonald's or Burger King—with their large budgets and legal staffs can figure out for each state how many hours the law allows a teenager to work and exactly what work a child may or may not do. Even a small business can with only a little effort determine what a particular employee is legally able to do. In addition, every business—indeed, every activity in society, from crossing the street to sitting in a movie theater—is guided by laws, restrictions, and customs. That is part of being part of a society.

Furthermore, these people say, laws are also ignored —deliberately broken. There have been cases when parents have telephoned their child's employer in the early morning hours to demand that the child be allowed to go home, but the child was not released until the work was done.

Reformers cite government reports and Operation Child Watch as proof of widespread violations of the present child labor laws. For example, the New York State Labor Department estimates that about 4,500 sweatshops in apparel industry firms operate in New York City alone, many of them illegally employing children.[11]

Hazards and Injuries

"Every year in this country, hundreds of children and teenagers are killed while working. Thousands more are maimed or seriously injured. The danger crosses social, economic and geographic lines: Middle-class suburban kids . . . can be just as much at risk as poor children. . . ."[12] So says an article in *Family Circle* magazine.

Reliable national statistics on the actual number of injured children are unavailable, but in testimony before Congress, Linda Golodner cited the American Academy of Pediatrics' estimate that 100,000 children are injured on the job each year, and said the figure doesn't "include children who are exposed to pesticides or herbicides or chemicals that may affect them in the future."[13]

Many reports on individual on-the-job incidents *are* available. A seventeen-year-old in Pennsylvania, for example, was killed while operating a compactor balling machine in a grocery store, a fifteen-year-old also from Pennsylvania was killed cleaning out a dough-mixing machine, and a thirteen-year-old Maryland boy lost his leg in a laundry extractor.[14] A fifteen-year-old in Alabama was killed while engaged in wrecking and demolition work, a sixteen-year-old in Texas was injured while operating hoisting equipment, a seventeen-year-old in Georgia was killed while removing the top of a hickory tree.[15]

Gung ho pro-youth-employment advocates do not deny such reports, but they tend to emphasize the positive. After all, people hurt themselves or get themselves killed all the time cooking breakfast, falling out of bed, crossing the street, etc.

Although no one wants to see children injured or killed on the job, interestingly, some parents are unconcerned about the possibility. For example, Jim McClure, director of guidance at the T. C. Williams High School in Alexandria, Virginia, remembers telling the mother of one of his students that he warned her son about using a dangerous electric meat slicer at work. Her response? "Why are you bothering him about this?"[16]

SHOULD RESTRICTIONS BE INCREASED OR REDUCED?

Probably both sides would agree that times have changed since the 1930s, when federal child labor laws were first enacted. And most people probably believe that when children work, society has an obligation to protect them from the dangers of child labor. However, the agreement stops there. While most people would agree that the laws need to be changed, the question is whether the laws need to become more restrictive or less.

Those who favor fewer restrictions minimize the abuses and point to the nation's need for labor and the benefits that working children receive.

In general, the sides divide between the pragmatic— represented usually by business, which wants fewer restrictions—and the ethical or moral, which wants better enforcement or more restrictions. It's not that business people are immoral or unethical; it's just that they often see things from a business perspective rather than from a humanitarian one.

One of the main issues revolves around the allowed number of hours children can work.

James M. Coleman, a spokesperson for the Food Service and Lodging Institute, a trade association whose member companies and franchises operate over 70,000 restaurants, fast-food chains, and lodging facilities, believes that the workday for fifteen-year-olds should be extended to 9:00 P.M. throughout the country. While trying to urge changes in federal law, he argued before the United States Congress that there was no difference between students working late and students staying up late to attend school functions. In fact, he said, school functions sometimes last far later than 9:00 P.M. The extension of the workday to nine o'clock would give fifteen-year-olds the opportunity of working a three-hour shift either in the afternoon from 3:00 to 6:00 or in the early evening from 6:00 to 9:00. Coleman contended that there was no difference between the shifts. Those who worked the early shift could study after work and those who worked the late shift could study earlier.[17]

Mark Gorman, a spokesperson for the National Restaurant Association, argues that "requiring fifteen-year-olds to stop work at 7:00 P.M.—right in the middle of the busy dinner hour—makes little sense.[18] Business executives who support extending the working hours of teens believe that teen work is crucial to business and when the labor market is tight some companies have "to hire fourteen- and fifteen-year-olds to keep the store open."[19]

Others disagree, saying that most teenagers after spending a full day in school are unlikely to go home and immediately begin studying and doing homework. Students need time to rest, eat, and just hang out. Educators argue that there *is* a difference between staying up late to participate in a musical program, a theatrical performance, or a sporting event, and staying up late to clean tables and wrap hamburgers. School activities, they say, offer intellectual, social, cultural, and physical growth opportunities that youth employment does not. Reformers add that meeting the needs of restaurant dinner crowds or shortening check-out lines in stores is not the responsibility of teenagers.

Reformers argue that without good laws, youth employment would quickly degenerate into child labor, with all the abuses and horrors of the past. Protection, they say, comes through laws and their enforcement. If the laws can't be enforced, then perhaps youth employment should be banned entirely. Otherwise, enforcement needs to be stepped up and made stricter.

A good example is the many child labor violations that continue to exist especially in modern sweatshops. Here recent-immigrant children work under conditions similar to those of a hundred years ago.[20] Many people believe that if the laws were more restrictive and the penalties large enough, such abuses would not occur.

The Child Labor Coalition—a group that includes such organizations as the American Academy of Pediatrics, American Federation of Teachers, Consumer Federation of America, General Federation of Women's Clubs, National Education Association, Children's Defense Fund, and various labor unions—wants Congress to enlarge the number of prohibited teenage occupations and work activities, reduce the number of hours children work, and vigorously enforce the laws with higher fines.

Reformers want to prohibit anyone under eighteen from selling door-to-door, driving school buses, or using power tools. They say that teens engaged in these activities are getting hurt and the government has the obligation to protect them. The business community replies that there is a labor shortage and young people are needed to fill these positions; if fines are increased, some businesses will no longer be able to afford to hire children.

In some ways the two sides are miles apart, since they never quite address the points of the other side. It seems as if the sides divide almost the same way the politcal parties divide, with Republicans tending to be probusiness and Democrats prolabor. The former sees issues often in terms of dollars and cents, the latter in terms of social obligations and responsibilities.

Which side are you on? Is it possible to support business/youth employment and not support child labor? Can you support shorter hours, compliance with existing laws, restriction of hazardous jobs while still being a capitalist?

TAKING RESPONSIBILITY

Since youth employment is probably here to stay and violations will never completely disappear, it is up to everyone involved to try to make the experience of youth employment a positive one. And although adults are still ultimately responsible for enforcing—or breaking—the laws, underage students can still take responsibility for making sure they are not abused or put into dangerous conditions.

Teenagers who choose to work can do a great deal to protect themselves in the work environment. They can inform themselves about child labor laws in their own state and find out what occupations and specific kinds of equipment they are not permitted to use. They can refuse to work "off the books" or more hours than the law allows. It would also help if students remember that they have more of an obligation to themselves and their own future than they have to their employers. Indeed, employers need the work of young people, as much if not more than the young people need the jobs. Students who know the law and stand up for their legal rights can wield the power to help stop child labor.

T E N

CHILD LABOR: A WORLD PROBLEM

The government makes laws for the poor and keeps them in the library.
  —Swami Agnivesh, India Daily Telegraph,
       October 4, 1985[1]

The United Nations heralded 1979 as the International Year of the Child. In that year the United Nations International Children's Emergency Fund (UNICEF); the International Labor Organization (ILO), an agency of the United Nations; the United Nations Commission on Human Rights; and the Anti-Slavery Society all examined on a global basis the exploited child worker. The investigations led to numerous reports that revealed the suffering of working children around the world. While the exploitation was far worse in some countries than in others, to some degree all left their working children unprotected.[2]

The number of abused working children was staggering. The *United Nations Special Report on the State of the*

World's Children estimated that more than 52 million children under the age of fifteen were working.[3] One year later, in 1980, the ILO revised upward the estimate to 100 million. The truth is that no one keeps records on children working illegally. The ILO believed the actual number of working children was probably *double* the official statistics.[4] In 1991 UNICEF estimated that "80 million children between the ages of ten and fourteen undertake work which is either so long or so onerous that it interferes with their normal development.[5]

The ILO found that all over the world children "toil long hours for a pittance and often under precarious and exploitive conditions." Employers hired children because they were "docile, fast, and agile" and "can be easily hired and fired and they cannot join unions."[6] Children who work under the worst conditions do so for personal and family survival and generally accept their role . . . (a role which turns them into) both the victim and the involuntary accomplice of an unjust situation."[7]

WHO ARE THE CHILDREN AND WHY DO THEY WORK?

Globally, most employed children come from poor families and generally from rural communities. Family poverty forces children into the workplace. In northeastern Thailand, for example, when the rice crop is inadequate, parents sell or lease their daughters. The parents do this in part because they believe it is better to sacrifice one child than the entire family. Parents use the money received from the sale of one child to help support the rest of the family.[8]

In India children are sometimes forced to work to pay off debts incurred by their parents or grandparents. The debts are incurred when adults borrow money to pay for life-cycle events like weddings. Since the celebrations are expensive and wages are low, the adults have difficulty

Homeless children in Guatemala City, Guatemala

paying back the loans, especially since interest rates are often extremely high. Forty percent interest is not unusual.[9] The parents in these circumstances are usually illiterate and do not understand that interest is the cost of borrowing the money and principal is the actual amount borrowed. Landowners encourage this kind of indebtedness. Children, grandchildren, and great-grandchildren work to pay off the debts of their forebears, and whole families remain in virtual slavery.[10] The system is called bonded slavery and is similar to the old European feudal system.

The feudal system in Europe lasted from the ninth to about the fifteenth century. In this political system people belonged to the land and the land belonged to the lord. Families were not free to leave the land and were required to pay the lord for the privilege of remaining there. The lord could charge whatever he pleased. The system is illegal today, in India as well as Europe. Nevertheless, in India it continues.

Poor parents who do not sell or lease their children may keep them within the family but push the young people into employment. The income the children earn may be the parents' only financial resource. It is not unusual for children to be able to find work when their parents cannot.[11]

Parents are not the only ones who control the lives of children. In India and South Africa, for example, older brothers sometimes mortgage siblings or their child brides.[12] The little girls work while their brothers receive the money.

Sometimes children enter the work force because they are kidnapped. This happens in places like Brazil, India, and South Africa.[13] In rural South Africa, for example, trucks drive through the black sections and pick up young girls. Bosses take away their identity papers and force the girls to work.[14]

Sometimes children work because there is no one to

take care of them. Poverty may be so severe that parents, unable to feed their children, simply abandon them to the streets and any work they can get. Other parents, instead of abandoning their children, try to better the lives of the family by emigrating. While emigration may bring some improvement, the family may find that they are almost as poor in the new country as they were in the old. Nine-and ten-year-old Turkish children, for example, work in Germany. Since neither the parents nor the youngsters are able to communicate in German, they are easily exploited in their new home.[15] The Anti-Slavery Society found Turkish children working in Belgian mines under deplorable conditions similar to those of eighteenth-century England.[16]

In Ethiopia and Uganda, 10 percent of the army consists of children under the age of fifteen. Some of the youngest soldiers are children of parents who were killed in war. The children are kind of a "mobile orphanage."[17] Military children generally come from the lowest socioeconomic group.[18] In some countries they may be as young as ten.

WHERE DO CHILDREN WORK?

Most children who work, work in agriculture. Indeed, children are a large part of the total agricultural work force around the world. Sometimes they work in groups with other children; sometimes they work within their own family unit. Crop-picking children have become an important element in filling the agricultural needs of the world.

Annually thousands of Mexican children migrate with their families to work in the growing fields of California. Children work on farms in India, Brazil, and South Africa, and the children of Argentina pick cotton and tobacco instead of going to school. Some of these working children may be as young as five or six years old. While many may work willingly, others are forced into labor.[19]

Farms are not the only place children work. In some countries like Italy and China human-rights investigators have found children working in factories doing various tasks, baking bread, making shoes, and building toys. They found them working in hotels as waiters, bellboys, and chambermaids. They saw them selling things in stores and serving and cleaning in restaurants and gas stations. In some countries children worked in the building trades, glass factories, and mines. Investigators found four-year-old Thai boys working in match factories.[20]

In Italy, children roll cigarettes and work in leather shops. There is in fact an "empire of clandestine work-shops" maintained by subcontractors who hire mostly children. In India, Pakistan, and Morocco children weave carpets. Around the world children sew, sell, pound, carry, and clean. Almost everywhere they work at street trades: cleaning shoes, guarding cars, and selling newspapers, magazines, flowers, and junk. Some do drug running, and others work as prostitutes. The Anti-Slavery Society dis-covered Turkish, Thai, and Moroccan children engaged in prostitution in Holland, France, and Germany as well as in their own countries.[21]

Many children work as soldiers and not all of them are orphans. In 1984 the United Nations reported that Iranian parents received money and discounts on food and mer-chandise if their child died in battle. It became quite prof-itable and honorable to lose a child. According to a 1986 UNICEF report, there is a growing trend in Africa, Asia, and Latin America to use child soldiers. Children serve in the armies of Iran and Iraq and in the guerrilla forces in Northern Ireland.[22]

WHAT ARE THE WORKING CONDITIONS?

No matter where a child works, the working conditions depend upon the character and mood of the employer. Some employers are generous; some are exploitive. No

Top: *Filipino boys making shoes*
Bottom: *Potters in Nepal*

one requires the employers give the children health insurance, fair hours, fair working conditions, fair pay, social security, or job security. There is no union support. When children work illegally, they fall outside the protection of the law; and adults often treat them with contempt, even when it is poverty that forces children to work.[23]

Farm children must labor long hours in the hot sun and frequently they ingest the pesticides used in the fields. In places like Argentina, India, and South Africa when children work in the same fields as their parents, only the parents are paid.[24] On Indian and South African farms, children are generally paid in food and clothing. Those who do receive cash earn half the adult wage.[25]

In South Africa the kidnapped children of course are not paid at all. They must either work or starve.[26] However, it is the ranchers of Brazil who have become notorious for their cruelty. In 1989, for example, eight Brazilian ranchers were accused of child slavery. Gerlom Alves da Silva, a teenager, and his younger brother Gernaldo were among a group of kidnapped children. Gerlom told the Pastoral Land Commission of the Roman Catholic church how he and the others were made to work on one ranch and then locked in ovens, beaten with electric cords, and made to sleep on the ground. In order to prevent the children from escaping, guards chained them to trees when they were not working.[27]

Although working conditions for children on farms are often terrible, the working conditions for children in other occupations across the world are also intolerable. In Berlin, Germany, for example, nine-and ten-year-old Turkish children work for Turkish employers in open-air markets starting as early as 4:30 A.M. Here again, the children are often paid in food rather than cash. During harvest time, hundreds of Turkish children in Germany work long days packing and unpacking fruits and vegetables. They clean, sort, and display them in the market. The work is illegal but common.[28]

When the Anti-Slavery Society visited leather shops in Italy they found working children as young as eight. The children worked nine to ten hours a day pasting soles and heels on shoes. Prolonged breathing of the toxic glue fumes and direct skin contact with the glue caused the disease known as glue polyneuritis. Polyneuritis results in paralysis of the upper and lower limbs and birth defects among the next generation of children. The society found similar conditions in leather shops in Spain. Such conditions prevail because the adult contractors set their own work standards of health and accident prevention.[29]

In the town of Satwarigaon, 12 miles (19 km) from New Delhi, India, children make bricks. Employers say that youngsters are better at it than adults. The children prepare the mixture, trample on it, then hand-mold it. The contractors pay the family, but the child is not paid. The work is hazardous to the child's health. Years of doing this work and inhaling the dust produces the lung diseases silicosis and tuberculosis. The children frequently injure their eyes and fingers.

The working conditions are even worse in the quarries of the Faridabad district in Haryana State, India. Children as young as six inhale the dust as they work in the quarries twelve hours a day in the hot sun. There is a shortage of drinking water, and both the children and their parents are intimidated by guards. Most of the families are in debt bondage and live in squalor. The alternative to this heavy work is starvation. Laws passed to protect the children are not enforced. The United Nations is working to change things, but changes come slowly.[30]

A team of investigators from the Anti-Slavery Society visited Morocco in 1975, 1977, and 1985. In 1975 they found girls as young as five years old working seventy-two hours a week making carpets. For years they breathed in the dust from carding and spinning machines. The noise was intolerable. In March the factory temperatures were so low that children had colds and sores on their faces.

Top: *A familiar scene on the streets of Mexico*
Bottom: *Young soldiers in
Uganda—aged seven and ten*

Working conditions caused eye and lung injuries. Children were given no more than two consecutive days off a year. By 1985 matters had improved, but only a little. The workday was cut to nine hours, and no one under six was employed.

Conditions in Indian carpet manufacturing are just as bad. In 1985 the Bonded Liberation Front rescued groups of kidnapped children from the carpet shed in the village of Mirzapur. There they found boys from six to ten years old forced to work from 4:00 A.M. until 2:00 P.M. Then, following a half-hour break and a meal of bread and lentils, the children were forced back to work until midnight. The bosses beat them with iron rods and bamboo, and the penalty for crying was getting hit with a stone tied to a cloth. When the children tried to run away, they were hung upside down from a tree and branded. When members of the Front returned to the area two years later they found that "nothing had changed."[31]

Many children around the world are taken into families as domestics. These household servants run errands and do the disagreeable home tasks, and since they live with their employers, they are on duty at all times. The number of working hours varies considerably with the job and the employer. A child may work from a few hours a day to fourteen. Girls in domestic service generally work extremely long hours.[32] Although this work arrangement is generally against the law, it is common practice in Latin America and parts of Asia and Africa.[33] Some people try to get around the law by calling it "adoption," but in reality the children are virtual household slaves. While honest adoption is socially desirable, domestic servitude is not.

In Mexico the legal working age is fourteen, yet an investigator found six- and seven-year-old girls cooking, cleaning, washing and ironing, and "baby-sitting" outside the family environment.[34] In 1980 Mauritania, a country along the western coast of Africa just north of Senegal, abolished slavery for the third time. Many of the slaves were children.[35]

IS THERE HOPE FOR THE FUTURE?

Children work for the same reasons adults work—for the income. Yet the wages children earn for their labor is considerably less than employed adults earn. Thus it is profitable for employers to hire children instead of adults. In Indonesia, for example, factory children receive 70 or 80 percent less than the adult wage.[36]

Children also work because they need something to do. In some countries outside the United States, like Italy, India, and the African nations, there are simply not enough schools for children to attend, even if they were not working. In India, fewer than 50 percent of children ages eleven to fourteen go to school even though school attendance is compulsory. The percentage is even lower in Asia and several countries in Latin America. Some families consider school a luxury or a waste of time.[37] Yet if children do not go to school they will never learn a trade or receive the education they need to improve their condition in life.

When children enter the labor market, they stimulate adult unemployment. This creates a vicious circle. The more adult unemployment, the more child labor and the more adult unemployment. Yet in Third World countries a dilemma exists. If the laws were actually enforced and children were kept out of the labor market, there would be widespread starvation and more abandoned children on the streets.[38] In the short run, according to even the best-informed people, "If the law against child labor were enforced, things will get worse rather than better. The reality is that either children work or they die of hunger along with their families."[39]

On the bright side, the United Nations is working to monitor, assist, and guide nations in identifying and solving child labor problems. It is working to attack poverty and prejudice, improve the educational system, and educate the public to the problems. The world body helps to arrange curative and preventive programs. Individual nations also are trying to protect children, but the problems are not easy to solve. Economically the world needs to have its children working, but at what age is a child too young to work? What work and what working conditions will the world find intolerable for children?

The ILO recommends that the minimum age for light work should be twelve to thirteen years old. For work that jeopardizes the health and morals of a young person, the ILO recommends eighteen as the minimum age. Recommendations, however, are not laws. Some countries agree to pass laws that follow these suggestions; some do not. But laws alone are not enough; someone has to enforce them.

Are the suggestions realistic? What will happen to families if the children are not permitted to work? Who will feed them? Who will do the unpleasant, dangerous work? What will happen to the world economy if cheap labor is no longer available? Will businesses be able to pay a living wage to all adults? What will children do if they don't work and there are not enough schools or recreational opportunities? Who will build schools and train teachers? Where will all this money come from? How do we start? To a greater or lesser degree, the whole world has the same problem. Perhaps the children of today will have the answers for tomorrow.

S O U R C E
N O T E S

CHAPTER ONE

1. Jonas Hanway, "A Sentimental History of Chimney Sweepers in London and Westminster, 1785," in Grace Abbott, *The Child and the State: Legal Status in the Family, Apprenticeship, and Child Labor: Select Documents with Introductory Notes,* vol. 1 (University of Chicago Press, 1938), p. 101.

2. *Journal of the House of Commons,* XLIII (28 George III, 1788), in ibid., pp. 104–106.

3. See Elias Mendelievich, ed., *Children at Work* (Geneva: International Labor Organization, 1979); Alec Fyfe, *Child Labour* (Cambridge, England: Polity Press, 1989); and Assefa Bequele and Jo Boyden, *Combating Child Labour* (Geneva: International Labour Office, 1988).

4. J. Aiken, "A Description of the Country from Thirty to Forty Miles Round Manchester, London, 1795," in Abbott, p. 106.

5. Ibid., pp. 21–42. See also Abbott, pp. 91–185.

6. "Resolutions for the Consideration of the Man-

chester Board of Health presented by Dr. Percival to the Manchester Board of Health, January 25, 1796," in Abbott, pp. 107–108.

7. Walter I. Trattner, *Crusade for the Children: A History of the National Child Labor Committee and Child Labor Reform in America* (Chicago: Quadrangle Books, 1970), p. 27.

8. Quoted in ibid., p. 23.

CHAPTER TWO

1. Lucy Larcom, *An Idyll of Work* (Boston, 1875), in Edith Abbott, "A Study of the Early History of Child Labor in America," *American Journal of Sociology,* vol. 14, July 1908, p. 37.

2. Grace Abbott, *The Child and the State: Legal Status in the Family, Apprenticeship, and Child Labor: Select Documents with Introductory Notes,* vol. 1 (Chicago: University of Chicago Press, 1938), pp. 189–212.

3. Edith Abbott, p. 21.

4. Grace Abbott, p. 272.

5. Ibid.

6. Ibid.

7. Ibid.

8. Edith Abbott, p. 32.

9. Walter I. Trattner, *Crusade for the Children: A History of the National Child Labor Committee and Child Labor Reform in America* (Chicago: Quadrangle Books, 1970), p. 31.

10. Report of the Massachusetts Bureau of Labor, 1870. See ibid., p. 34.

11. Ibid, pp. 29–31. This report describes one instrument for whipping children as an "eighteen inch leather strap with tacks driven through the striking end."

12. Ibid., pp. 30–35.

13. *Mechanics Free Press* (August 21, 1830), in Grace Abbott, p. 279.

14. Edith Abbott, p. 29.

15. Grace Abbott, p. 276.

16. Edith Abbott, p. 33.

17. Trattner, p. 37.

18. Jeremy P. Felt, *Hostages of Fortune: Child Labor Reform in New York State* (Syracuse [N.Y.] University Press, 1965), p. 3.

19. Trattner, pp. 40, 252.

20. Ibid., p. 81.

21. Ibid., p. 40.

22. Ibid., p. 3. See also Edith Abbott, p. 27. Statistics on the extent of child labor in the nineteenth century are unreliable. One report states that about 500 men and 3,500 women were employed nationwide in cotton mills in 1811. The Committee on Manufacturing reported 24,000 boys under seventeen and 66,000 women and girls out of an estimated 100,000 cotton mill employees. According to another report, 30 percent of all the cotton workers of the South were children. See Johnsen, p. 77.

23. Nettie P. McGill, *Child Workers on City Streets*, (Washington, D.C.: U.S. Government Printing Office, United States Department of Labor, Children's Bureau, 1928), p. 3.

24. Ibid., p. 4.

25. Ibid., p. 5.

26. Ibid., pp. 13–14, 47.

27. Ibid., p. 41.

28. Ibid., p. 31.

29. Grace Abbott, pp. 398–404.

30. Nina Rosenblum, director, and Daniel Allentuck, writer, *America and Lewis Hine*, video, 56 minutes (New York: Daedalus Productions, Inc., 1984).

31. Ibid.

32. Alan Trachtenberg, *America & Lewis Hine: Photographs, 1904–1940* (Millerton, N.Y.: Brooklyn Museum/ Aperture, 1977), p. 84.

33. Grace Abbott, pp. 362–363, 388.

CHAPTER THREE

1.Julia E. Johnsen, *Selected Articles on Child Labor* (New York: H. W. Wilson, 1925), p. 79.

2. Jeremy P. Felt, *Hostages of Fortune: Child Labor Reform in New York State* (Syracuse, N.Y.: Syracuse University Press, 1965), p. 18.

3. Ibid., p. 19.

4. Walter I. Trattner, *Crusade for the Children: A History of the National Child Labor Committee and Child Labor Reform in America* (Chicago: Quadrangle Books, 1970), p. 52.

5. Elizabeth Sands Johnson, "Child Labor Legislation," in John R. Commons, *History of Labor in the United States, 1896–1932*, vol. 3 (New York: Macmillan, 1935; reprint, August M. Kelley, 1966), p. 406, and Trattner, p. 80.

6. Trattner, p. 54. See also Grace Abbott, *The Child and the State: Legal Status in the Family, Apprenticeship, and Child Labor: Select Documents with Introductory Notes*, vol. 1 (University of Chicago Press, 1938), pp. 64–65.

7. Ibid.

8. Johnson, p. 409.

9. Ibid., pp. 187–190. The list of children's occupations in southern textile mills goes on for four pages.

10. Quoted in Katharine DuPre Lumpkin and Dorothy Wolff Douglas, *Child Workers in America* (New York: Robert M. McBride, 1937), p. 219.

11. Johnson, p. 414.

12. Lumpkin and Douglas, p. 219.

13. Johnson, p. 413.

14. Trattner, pp. 77–78.

15. Johnson, p. 411.

16. Ibid., p. 412.

17. Ibid., p. 423.

CHAPTER FOUR

1. Alan Trachtenberg, *America & Lewis Hine: Photographs, 1904–1940* (Millerton, N.Y.: Brooklyn Museum/Aperture, 1977), p. 129.

2. Ibid., p. 58.

3. Verna Posever Curtis and Stanley Mallach, *Photography and Reform: Lewis Hine & The National Child Labor Committee* (Milwaukee: Milwaukee Art Museum: 1984), p. 65.

4. Trachtenberg, pp. 13, 58. See also Nina Rosenblum, director, and Daniel Allentuck, writer, *America and Lewis Hine,* video, 56 minutes (New York: Daedalus Productions, 1984).

5. Grace Abbott, *The Child and the State: Legal Status in the Family, Apprenticeship, and Child Labor: Select Documents with Introductory Notes,* vol. 1 (Chicago: University of Chicago Press, 1938), p. 374.

6. Julia E. Johnsen, *Selected Articles on Child Labor* (New York: H.W. Wilson, 1925), pp. 94–96.

7. Abbott, p. 375.

8. Trachtenberg, p. 129.

9. Curtis and Mallach, p. 38.

10. Ibid., p. 56.

11. Trachtenberg, p. 84.

12. Curtis and Mallach, p. 41.

13. Lewis W. Hine, "Sugarbeet Children in Wisconsin," July 1915, *National Child Labor Committee Pamphlet,* p. 1, in ibid., p. 23.

14. Judith Mara Gutman, *Lewis W. Hine and the American Social Conscience* (New York: Walker, 1967), p. 3.

CHAPTER FIVE

1. Quoted in Walter I. Trattner, *Crusade for the Children: A History of the National Child Labor Committee*

and Child Labor Reform in America (Chicago: Quadrangle Books, 1970), p. 199.

2. Ibid., p. 91.

3. Elizabeth Sands Johnson, "Child Labor Legislation," in John R. Commons, *History of Labor in the United States, 1896–1932*, vol. 3 (New York: Macmillan, 1935; reprint, August M. Kelley, 1966), p. 441.

4. Trattner, p. 159.

5. Ibid., p. 160.

6. Elizabeth Brandeis, "Labor Legislation," in John R. Commons, *History of Labor in the United States, 1896–1932*, vol. 3 (New York: Macmillan, 1935; reprint 1966), pp. 694–695.

7. Johnson, p. 443.

8. Ibid., pp. 445–446; and also Grace Abbott, *The Child and the State: Legal Status in the Family, Apprenticeship, and Child Labor: Select Documents with Introductory Notes,* vol. 1 (Chicago: University of Chicago Press, 1938), pp. 532–533.

9. Johnson, p. 448.

10. Trattner, p. 172.

11. Grace Abbott, p. 558.

12. Trattner, p. 196.

13. Ibid., p. 198.

14. Ibid, p. 200.

15. Ibid., p. 202.

16. Ibid., p. 207.

17. Katharine DuPre Lumpkin and Dorothy Wolff Douglas, *Child Workers in America* (New York: Robert M. McBride, 1937), p. 219, and Ronald B. Taylor, *Sweatshops in the Sun: Child Labor on the Farm* (Boston: Beacon Press, 1973), p. 151.

18. Taylor, p. 158.

19. Ibid., pp. 148–152, 209–230, and Grace Abbott, pp. 564–597.

20. Trattner, pp. 215, 301.

21. Ibid., p. 216.

22. Ibid., p. 220.

23. Ibid., p. 218.

24. Ella A. Merritt and Floyd Hendricks, "Trend of Child labor, 1940–1944," *Monthly Labor Review*, vol. 60 (April 1945), pp. 756–775.

25. Trattner, p. 218, and Ellen Greenberger and Laurence Steinberg, *When Teenagers Work: The Psychological and Social Costs of Adolescent Employment* (New York: Basic Books, 1986), p. 59.

26. United States General Accounting Office, *Child Labor: Increases in Detected Child Labor Violations Throughout the United States* (Washington, D.C.: U.S. Government Printing Office, 1990), pp. 48–50.

CHAPTER SIX

1. Ellen Greenberger and Laurence Steinberg, *When Teenagers Work: The Psychological and Social Costs of Adolescent Employment* (New York: Basic Books, 1986), p. 11.

2. Ibid., pp. 18–20.

3. Ibid., p. 179.

4. Ibid., pp. 34–37.

5. *New York Times*, December 10, 1989, section 1, p. 1.

6. *Weekend Edition,* National Public Radio, June 16, 1990, Susan Leffler, reporter. See also *New York Times*, March 15, 1990, p. A8.

7. United States General Accounting Office, *"Sweatshops" in New York City: A Local Example of a Nationwide Problem,* (Washington, D.C.: U.S. Government Printing Office, June 1989), pp. 8, 23.

8. Kendall J. Willis, "Garment Sweatshops Are Spreading," *New York Times,* September 6, 1987, section 1, p. 38.

9. Philip Landrigan, Testimony on the Hazards to

Children of Industrial Homework, before the United States House of Representatives Committee on Education and Labor, Discussing Hazards to Children of Industrial Homework, March 29, 1989.

10. Willis, p. 38.

11. Ibid.

12. Landrigan.

13. United States General Accounting Office, *"Sweatshops" in New York City: A Local Example of a Nationwide Problem,* pp. 30–33.

14. Terrence Falk, "Fast Foods," *Milwaukee,* vol. 14, no. 11, November 1989, pp. 63 ff.

15. *Los Angeles Times,* May 1, 1989, section IV, p. 5.

CHAPTER SEVEN

1. Susan H. Pollack, Philip J. Landrigan, and David L. Mallino, "Child Labor in 1990: Prevalence and Health Hazards," *Annual Review of Public Health, 1990,* vol. 11, p. 369.

2. Rosalind Wright, "The Hidden Cost of Child Labor," *Family Circle* (March 12, 1991), p. 88.

3. Ronald B. Taylor, *Sweatshops in the Sun: Child Labor on the Farm* (Boston: Beacon Press, 1973), p. 122.

4. Ibid., p. 183.

5. Statement of Raymond M. Wheeler, M.D., Internist, Charlotte, to the Senate Migrant Labor Subcommittee. See Ibid., p. 157. N.C., in "Migrant and Seasonal Farmworker Powerlessness," Part 8-A, pp. 4980–4993. See also Taylor, p. 169.

6. Taylor, p. 5.

7. Alec Fyfe, *Child Labour* (Cambridge, England: Polity Press, 1989), p. 64.

8. Statement of Linda F. Golodner, Executive Director, National Consumers League, Co-Chair, Child Labor Coalition, before the Subcommittee on Labor Standards

of the Committee on Education and Labor, United States House of Representatives, August 1, 1990.

9. Taylor, pp. 150–178.

10. Ibid., pp. 14, 24–25.

11. Golodner.

12. Pollack et al., p. 361.

13. Golodner.

14. *American Journal of Diseases of Children*, American Medical Association, as reported by *New York Times*, December 8, 1987, part A, p. 18.

15. *Wall Street Journal*, September 5, 1989, part A, p. 1.

16. Wright, p. 134.

17. Ibid.

18. Goldoner, p. 3.

19. *Wall Street Journal*, September 5, 1989, p. 1.

CHAPTER EIGHT

1. *New York Times*, February 5, 1990, p. B4, and March 10, 1990, p. 8.

2. Froma Joselow, "Why Business Turns to Teenagers," *New York Times*, March 26, 1989, business section, p. 1.

3. *Philadelphia Inquirer*, May 14, 1989.

4. Don Colburn, "Teenaged Farm Workers Suffer Hearing Loss," *Washington Post*, June 6, 1989, *Health*, p. 5.

5. Speech delivered by the Honorable William C. Brooks, Assistant Secretary for Employment Standards, United States Department of Labor, before the Child Labor Advisory Committee, February 7, 1990, Washington, D.C.

6. United States General Accounting Office, *Child Labor: Increases in Detected Child Labor Violations Throughout the United States* (Washington, D.C.: U.S. Government Printing Office, 1990), p. 14.

7. *New York Times,* March 16, 1990, p. A11.

8. *Child Labor,* p. 3.

9. Ibid., p. 22.

10. Ibid, p. 25.

11. Ibid., pp. 45–50.

12. *Child Labor,* p. 23.

13. Brooks.

14. *Child Labor,* p. 24.

15. *New York Times,* February 8, 1990, A22.

16. Testimony of James M. Coleman, General Counsel for the Foodservice and Lodging Institute, before the Labor Standards Subcommittee of the House Education and Labor Committee, July 19, 1990.

CHAPTER NINE

1. Statement of Rudolph A. Oswald, Director, Department of Economic Research, American Federation of Labor and Congress of Industrial Organizations before the subcommittee on Labor Standards of the Committee on Education and Labor, U.S. House of Representatives, on the Young American Workers' Bill of Rights, on June 28, 1990, p. 5.

2. Ellen Greenberger and Laurence Steinberg, *When Teenagers Work: The Psychological and Social Costs of Adolescent Employment* (New York: Basic Books, 1986), pp. 90–155.

3. Ibid., pp. 208ff.

4. Ibid., pp. 216–218.

5. *New York Times,* June 11, 1989, p. 40.

6. Telephone interview with Geoffrey Greene, Philadelphia, Pa., September 3, 1991.

7. Testimony of James M. Coleman, General Counsel for the Foodservice and Lodging Institute, before the Labor Standards Subcommittee of the House Education and Labor Committee, July 19, 1990, p. 2.

8. Froma Joselow, "Why Business Turns to Teen-Agers," *New York Times,* March 26, 1989, p. 1.

9. Statement of Mark Gorman, Senior Director, Government Affairs, National Restaurant Association, before the House Subcommittee on Labor Standards, Child Labor Reform, July 19, 1990, pp. 3–5.

10. Coleman, p. 3.

11. General Accounting Office, *"Sweatshops" in New York City: A Local Example of a Nationwide Problem* (Washington, D.C.: U.S. Government Printing Office, 1989), p. 2.

12. Rosalind Wright, "The Hidden Cost of Child Labor," *Family Circle,* March 12, 1991, p. 83.

13. Testimony of Linda F. Golodner, Executive Director, National Consumers League Co-Chair, Child Labor Coalition, before the Subcommittee on Labor Standards of the Committee on Education and Labor, U.S. House of Representatives, August 1, 1990, p. 3.

14. Wright, pp. 84–86.

15. General Accounting Office, *Child Labor: Increases in Detected Child Labor Violations Throughout the United States* (Washington, D.C.: U.S. Government Printing Office, 1990), pp. 45–51.

16. Joselow, p. 1.

17. Coleman, p. 5.

18. Gorman, p. 5.

19. Joselow, p. 1.

20. *Sweatshops in New York City,* pp. 8–10.

CHAPTER TEN

1. Quoted in Alec Fyfe, *Child Labour* (Cambridge, England: Polity Press, 1989), p. 77.

2. Elias Mendelievich, ed., *Children at Work* (Geneva: International Labor Organization, 1979). See also William James Knight, *The World's Exploited Children: Growing*

Up Sadly, monograph 4 (Washington, D.C.: United States Department of Labor, Bureau of International Labor Affairs, March 1980).

3. Elias Mendelievich, "Child Labour," *International Labor Review,* vol. 18, no. 5, September-October 1979, p. 557.

4. *Los Angeles Times,* June 28, 1988, IV, p. 21. See also Susan H. Pollack, Philip J. Landrigan, and David L. Mallino, "Child Labor in 1990: Prevalence and Health Hazards," *Annual Review of Public Health, 1990,* vol. 11, p. 371.

5. *The State of the World's Children 1991* (New York: Oxford University Press, for UNICEF), p. 42.

6. Ibid.

7. Mendelievich, *Children at Work,* p. 5.

8. Roger Sawyer, *Children Enslaved* (London: Routledge, 1988), p. 107.

9. Ibid., p. 56.

10. Ibid., p. 50.

11. Mendelievich, *Children at Work,* p. 35.

12. Sawyer, p. 53.

13. Fyfe, p. 82.

14. Ibid.

15. Sawyer, p. 106.

16. Ibid., p. 119.

17. Fyfe, pp. 85–87.

18. Ibid., p. 83.

19. Sawyer, p. 106.

20. Ibid., p. 107.

21. Fyfe, p. 119.

22. Ibid., p. 83.

23. Mendelievich, *Children at Work,* pp. 35, 95.

24. Sawyer, p. 106.

25. Ibid., pp. 48–50.

26. Fyfe, p. 82.

27. *New York Times,* September 6, 1990, p. A10.

28. Sawyer, p. 106.

29. Ibid., pp. 122–125.

30. Ibid., p. 56.
31. Ibid., pp. 114–116.
32. Mendelievich, *Children at Work,* pp. 36–37.
33. Ibid., pp. 35–36.
34. Ibid., p. 102.
35. Sawyer, p. 24.
36. Mendelievich, *Children at Work,* p. 89.
37. Ibid., pp. 51–52.
38. Ibid., p. 51.
39. Knight, p. 13.

S E L E C T E D
BIBLIOGRAPHY

BOOKS

Abbott, Grace. *The Child and the State: Legal Status in the Family, Apprenticeship and Child Labor: Select Documents with Introductory Notes*. Vol. 1. Chicago: University of Chicago Press, 1938.

Bequele, Assefa, and Jo Boyden, eds. *Combating Child Labour*. Geneva: International Labour Organization, 1988.

Felt, Jeremy P. *Hostages of Fortune: Child Labor Reform in New York State*. Syracuse, N.Y.: Syracuse University Press, 1965.

Fyfe, Alec. *Child Labour* Cambridge, England: Polity Press, 1989.

Greenberger, Ellen, and Laurence Steinberg. *When Teenagers Work: The Psychological and Social Costs of Adolescent Employment*. New York: Basic Books, 1986.

Gutman, Judith Mara. *Lewis W. Hine and the American Social Conscience*. New York: Walker, 1967.

Johnson, Elizabeth Sands. "Child Labor Legislation," in John R. Commons, ed., *History of Labor in the United States: 1896–1932*. Vol. 3. New York: Macmillan, 1935. Reprint New York: August M. Kelley, 1966.

Johnson, Julia E. *Selected Articles on Child Labor.* New York: H.W. Wilson, 1925.

Lumpkin, Katharine Dupre, and Dorothy Wolff Douglas. *Child Workers in America.* New York: Robert M. McBride, 1937.

McGill, Nettie. *Child Workers on City Streets.* Washington, D.C.: U.S. Government Printing Office, United States Department of Labor, Children's Bureau, 1928.

Mendelievich, Elias, ed. *Children at Work.* Geneva: International Labor Organization, 1979.

Nasaw, David. *Children of the City: At Work and at Play.* Garden City, N.Y.: Anchor Press/Doubleday, 1985.

Peck, Robert Newton. *Arly.* New York: Walker, 1989. (A young-adult novel.)

Sawyer, Roger. *Children Enslaved.* London: Routledge: 1988.

Taylor, Ronald. *Sweatshops in the Sun: Child Labor on the Farms.* Boston: Beacon Press, 1973.

Trachtenberg, Alan. *America and Lewis Hine: Photographs: 1904–1940.* Millerton, N.Y.: Brooklyn Museum/Aperture, 1977.

Trattner, Walter I. *Crusade for the Children: A History of the National Child Labor Committee and Child Labor Reform in America.* Chicago: Quandrangle Books, 1970.

ARTICLES

Abbott, Edith. "A Study of the Early History of Child Labor in America." *American Journal of Sociology,* 14 (July 1908), pp. 15–37.

Falk, Terrence. "Late Night in Fast Foods." *Milwaukee* 14 (November 14, 1989), pp. 63 ff.

Joselow, Froma. "Why Business Turns to Teenagers." *New York Times,* business section, March 26, 1989, p. 1.

Merritt, Ella A., and Floyd Hendricks. "Trend of Child Labor: 1940–1944." *Monthly Labor Review* 60 (April 1945), pp. 756–775.

Miller, Annetta. "Work and What It's Worth." *Newsweek* Special Issue, summer/fall 1990, pp. 28–33.

Pollack, Susan H., Phillip J. Landrigan, and David L. Mallino. "Child Labor in 1990: Prevalence and Health Hazards." *Annual Review of Public Health* 11 (1990) pp. 359–375.

GOVERNMENT DOCUMENTS

United States General Accounting Office. *Child Labor: Increases in Detected Child Labor Violations Throughout the United States.* Washington, D.C.: U.S. Government Printing Office, April 1990.

————. *"Sweatshops" in New York City: A Local Example of a Nationwide Problem.* June 1989.

CONGRESSIONAL TESTIMONY

Coleman, James M. Statement of James M. Coleman, General Counsel for the Foodservice and Lodging Institute, before the Labor Standards Subcommittee of the House Education and Labor Committee, July 19, 1990.

Golodner, Linda F. Statement of Linda F. Golodner, Executive Director, National Consumers League, Co-Chair, Child Labor Coalition, before the Subcommittee on Labor Standards of the Committee on Education and Labor, United States House of Representatives, August 1, 1990.

Gorman, Mark. Statement of Mark Gorman, Senior Director, Government Affairs, National Restaurant Association, before the House Subcommittee on Labor Standards, Child Labor Reform, July 19, 1990.

Landrigan, Philip. Testimony of Philip Landrigan on the Hazards to Children of Industrial Homework, before the United States House of Representatives Committee on Education and Labor, March 29, 1989.

I N D E X